Contents

Acknowledgments   v

Welcome   1

Chapter 1
Beginning Your Journey   5

Chapter 2
Building a Strong Foundation   23

Chapter 3
Connecting with Women Friends   43

Chapter 4
Creating Clarity   57

Chapter 5
Embracing Independence   75

Chapter 6
Reclaiming Your Vision   93

Chapter 7
Generating Energy   105

Chapter 8
Constructing a Transformative Plan   121

Chapter 9
Taking Action   131

Chapter 10
Relating to Men Again   145

Conclusion
An Incredible Destination   159

Bibliography   165

Transformational
Divorce

Discover Yourself, Reclaim Your Dreams,

& Embrace Life's Unlimited Possibilities

Karen Kahn Wilson, Ed.D.

NEW HARBINGER PUBLICATIONS, INC.

Publisher's Note

This publication is designed to provide accurate and authoritative information in regard to the subject matter covered. It is sold with the understanding that the publisher is not engaged in rendering psychological, financial, legal, or other professional services. If expert assistance or counseling is needed, the services of a competent professional should be sought.

Distributed in Canada by Raincoast Books

Copyright © 2003 by Karen Kahn Wilson
New Harbinger Publications, Inc.
5674 Shattuck Avenue
Oakland, CA 94609

Cover design by Poulson-Gluck Designs
Edited by Jueli Gastwirth
Text design by Michele Waters

ISBN 1-57224-341-4 Paperback

All Rights Reserved

Printed in the United States of America

New Harbinger Publications' Web site address: www.newharbinger.com

05 04 03

10 9 8 7 6 5 4 3 2 1

First printing

Acknowledgments

This book represents the fulfillment of one of my life dreams: the gathering together of my thoughts and experiences into a guide that I hope will make a difference in the lives of women who are walking where I have walked as a divorced woman. I am able to call myself "an author" because of the special, loving, and supportive people who have surrounded me for many years. I celebrate the opportunity to be able to thank them in this public format.

I have never had a chance to thank the woman who encouraged me to be a psychologist. I hope that these words will somehow find their way to her. Ann Robinson was my psychology professor at Trinity College in Connecticut in 1971. She pulled me aside during a class break and said, "You should be a psychologist." Psychology and coaching have been my constant companions ever since. Ann, you were my first mentor and I will be eternally grateful.

Next, I want to thank the midwife of this project, Jueli Gastwirth, Senior Acquisitions Editor at New Harbinger Publications. Thank you for making this dream a reality. Your belief in what I had to say enabled my thoughts to flow.

My closest friend, Jane Herring-Choate, the woman with whom I have walked my divorce journey, has been at the heart of everything that I have written. You have taught me about integrity, heart, and sisterhood. You are the best and I thank you. Char Tosi, I thank you for offering me your gentle and wise spirit in friendship as well as teaching me about how women can connect to others from the deepest places of their being. To Maud Purcell, whom I have known since the college years, thank you for reminding me that true friendship never dies, despite time and distance, and for appearing with encouragement and possibilities when I needed it most.

I thank my friends, Meg Gannon, Eve Poling, Tom Muha, and Diana Clancy, for making space in your busy schedules to listen to my exhaustion, affirm my message, challenge me when I needed it, and nurture me when I was depleted.

Thanks to my coach, wise woman Cathie Siders, for helping me get organized and create the space to be energized, creative, and productive and for reminding me that an irreverent sense of humor is important.

To Rudy Bauer, my therapist for many, many years: thank you for stepping out of your usual way of working and helping me discover my uniqueness and strength.

I thank Eleanor Craig Greene for being a wonderful model of an author and mentor. Your e-mails of encouragement were gems that brightened my day. Heather, thank you for coming into my life with love, acceptance, an open spirit, and for bringing Burl and Isaac with you. My life is much richer because you are a part of my family.

Meg, I treasure your support, your exuberance, and the way you embrace those you love.

To the women of Women Coaching Women who are open to new ways of serving women, and the women who visit DivorcedLiving.com, I thank you for contributing your voices and hearts.

I have been blessed in having had many "teachers" who have helped me transform my life. I want to thank all of you: the men I have met (especially the ones who "rejected" me), my clients, and the women from Woman Within. Also to the many writers who have expanded my way of thinking about myself, others, and the world—thank you.

My family is the core of who I am. I thank my sister and brother, Shoshi Kahn-Woods and Dan Kahn, for checking on me often and always having a place for me at their tables. I cannot thank my father without bursting into tears. His death in 1984 left a huge space within me, yet now his spirit fills me with belief in myself, family, and love, and a drive to make a contribution to the world. Mom, you will always be my model of a strong woman who finds energy, drive, love, and curiosity even when the world seems dark. You have created a safety net of love in which I could find myself, and you have never stopped believing in me. I can never thank you enough for all that you are and all that you have given to me.

I want to thank my golden retriever, Annie, who has lovingly sat under my feet as I have written each word of this book. I am sure we have spent many lifetimes together.

And, Charlie, my life partner. Thank you for waiting to enter my life until I was ready to truly love and be loved. You continue to help me learn about that fragile dance of intimacy and independence that is a center point of my growth. I thank you for each time you hug me, each time you call me, each time you say, "You can do it," when I don't think I can. You continue to teach me about partnership, integrity, and giving. I always knew you were out there. Thank you for finding me and loving me.

I am filled with gratitude to those named and unnamed who have been a part of my incredible journey. Because of your presence in my life, I have the daily joy of discovering new possibilities and am able to embrace life with excitement and wonder. This book is one of my "stepping stones." Thank you all for light, faith, and love.

Welcome

Dear Reader,

Welcome to *Transformational Divorce*. Thank you for choosing this book to help you on your journey.

I hope this book will be an experience for you, not just a source of information. My image is that each time a woman picks up this book she is magically connected with others who are reading and have read *Transformational Divorce*. This means that you are not alone—other divorced and separated women who have asked similar questions and have grappled with similar problems join you: Women who have had moments of feeling emotions similar to yours, such as confusion, disorientation, anger, sadness, hopelessness, loneliness, fear (lots of fear), and uncertainty; women in similar circumstances to yours who've experienced excitement, optimism, energy, relief, creativity, powerfulness, and strength. A woman's healing begins when she feels connected, when she feels that she belongs to a group and knows that she is not different or strange. A woman's healing begins when she knows that she shares a struggle similar to that of many other women.

This book is not only about *healing* from the wounds of divorce. It is about *transformation* that extends beyond the bounds of recovery. Healing is a mechanism that returns a wound from cut, bruised, or bleeding to its original, maybe slightly scarred, condition. A spot once injured, for example, is restored to functional. Transformation, on the other hand, is an active process that allows for expansion beyond healing. An object that is transformed is changed, altered, and modified. It sheds its original appearance and adopts a new shape or a new function. A caterpillar transforms into a butterfly; a gawky teenager transforms into a powerful woman. When you heal, you return to where you were before your injury. When you transform, you can grow in any direction. When you divorce, you are faced with an important choice: whether to heal, recover, and reestablish your life's equilibrium to your premarital state of being (without a partner), or to become engaged in the process of transformation and use the experience of divorce as a catalyst to propel you into new directions, explore your potential as a woman, and expand your world, your life, your being.

The contemplation of this choice is a very profound task. Transformation will require effort, risk, and patience. It's a ride on an emotional roller coaster that may make you feel sick on one day and exhilarated the next. Creating positive change may require that you dramatically alter the way you approach life and the people in your life. It may require that you learn to think, act, and react differently, and that you reject former ways of thinking. It may require that you develop new ways of feeling, believing, acting, connecting, speaking, dressing, laughing, crying, dancing, spending, working, playing, and more. Are you willing to walk this sometimes-uncomfortable passage from what was to what may be?

If you answer yes, it is important to remember that you will have choices all along the way. There is no one way that you "should" or "must" be. There are no standards, no rules. This is about your life. You have choices about how you live, the people with whom you live, the values you hold dear, and how quickly you want to implement change. In addition, know that you are not alone. In having read this letter, you are now a part of a large and growing group of women who are choosing to "do their lives" differently, who are opting to use divorce as the push that they have needed to live vibrant, meaningful, exciting lives. They are finding new possibilities and creating new futures; they're reclaiming their dreams and making them realities.

It's difficult to write a book that equally applies to everyone. So, I sadly had to make some choices about what segment of the population to address, knowing that this slant might exclude others. I have chosen to direct the content and exercises toward women who were in heterosexual marriages. While the material is particularly relevant for this specific group, I hope that women ending same-sex relationships as well as all men also will find the model and concepts helpful. I am sorry to have excluded you in my written voice. I do include you in my thoughts.

This book comes from my heart. It comes from my own passion for living and growing. It comes from a commitment that I made to myself (before I was born, if that's possible) to live life joyfully, to live life in a way that was consistent with my wants and values, and to keep on walking, learning, and growing even when the path was bumpy and difficult (and believe me those times have been there).

I welcome you to this book. I hope it provides you with the mechanisms to contemplate your choices, to develop new visions for yourself and your future, and to create a life for yourself that makes you feel alive, empowered, and loved.

—Karen Kahn Wilson
Bethesda, Maryland
2003

Chapter 1

Beginning Your Journey

What happened to your dreams? How many times as a child were you asked, "What do you want to be when you grow up?" Take a moment and think about all the different responses that you gave when you were a growing girl. Did you want to be a kindergarten teacher? A sports coach? An ambassador? A chef? The President of the United States? What memories come up for you? Dreams and aspirations are at their creative peak between nine and twelve years of age. They seem to quiet down during the social years of your early teens, when a new vision of the future comes to mind: the vision of being in a forever relationship with a man. Then, at the age of thirteen or so, most women find themselves caught in the bind of having to hold two dreams: that of being a dynamic, independent woman, and the vision of being connected to a man. The complication of having these two visions plagues many women for the rest of their lives.

Why do women often choose to become more entranced with the fantasy of a connection with a significant man rather than with other aspirations? Most likely because of women's "psychological DNA," their inner wiring, which propels them to seek deep, meaningful, connections with others (men and women). Some researchers say this urge to connect is stronger than the drive to be independent (Miller 1997).

What Do You Want to Be When You Grow Up?

So what happened to your dreams of being an artist or a writer or an executive? Were they hidden by an intense desire to be in a lasting connection with another person? Tragically, you may have spent so much time and energy striving to satisfy your need for meaningful connection, that most, even all, of your creative visions to impact the world with your individual talent were lost and forgotten.

And now you are divorced and on your own. The significant connection for which you strived for so long is severed. Where are you now? Faced with the same old question: "What do you want to be when you grow up?" Do you draw a blank when asked this question? Try remembering how you answered it when you were a child.

The return to "What do you want to be when you grow up?" is great news. You have new possibilities, another chance. If it doesn't feel this way to you, that's normal. Most women become very frightened when they become separated and divorced. Think about it: you have spent all of these years "working" to answer your primary inner calling—connection—and now you are back on your own. Of course you are afraid. This fear is even larger than you may have realized. (Contrary to what people around you may be saying, you are not crazy or "blowing this 'thing' out of proportion.") Eventually, this book will help you to explore fear in detail, but for right now, let's focus on where you are standing when your relationship ends.

Standing at the Crossroads

Imagine yourself walking down a road. The name of the road on which you've been traveling is "Marriage Highway." You're standing at a stop sign. Many new roads branch off from this location. You have choices, choices that you did not have when you were younger. You now have life experience, which makes you an older and wiser traveler (although it might not always feel this way).

As you stand at this crossroads with your marriage behind you, all kinds of directions and paths are now open and available. You have the opportunity to transform your life. You have the opportunity to revisit the question about what you want to be when you grow up, and consider it from the vantage point of a mature woman. You have the opportunity to dust off old hopes and dreams and make them realities. You have the opportunity to transform the experience of divorce—an event that holds many hostage to past disappointments—and turn it into an event that propels you into a future of unlimited possibilities. You can choose to transform your experience of divorce from a potentially life-debilitating event into an event that is life enhancing.

Because divorce brings the life that you had been living to a screeching halt, in effect causing the death of what was, the end of your relationship enables you to give birth to new inner clarity and strength. This book will provide you with ideas and experiences that will jump-start your own path of rebirth and transformation. You can create a wonderful life when you give yourself permission to reflect on what was, contemplate what can be, and take action to bring your visions into everyday reality.

How to Read This Book

This is not another divorce-recovery book that teaches you merely how to cope. Coping is not enough; coping maintains life as you have known it. This is also not another heal-through-finding-love-again book. Finding a new mate isn't the right choice for everyone. Mates only represent one piece of who you are and what the future can hold. This book is about rediscovering all of who you are as a woman. It's about picking up the pieces of your dreams that may have been forgotten during your dating and marital years, and creating a future that is fuller, happier, and more meaningful than ever before.

In the chapters ahead, you will learn to grow from the past, think about yourself and your life in new ways, create exciting visions of your future, develop a map for the journey ahead, and implement well-thought-out actions that will move you into a phenomenal tomorrow. Try not to use this book as just another piece of information that you consider for a moment and then set aside. Use this book actively. Read it straight through—chapter by chapter—and complete the exercises as they are presented. It may be helpful to imagine that you are at a workshop where you are personally being guided. Moving through the material in sequential order will maximize your learning and allow you to experience a powerful unfolding process within yourself.

Active Participation

You're encouraged to interact with this book. That is, agree with it, disagree with it, and most important of all, use it actively. Pick up a highlighter, some "sticky notes," a pen, and a journal. When you read a passage that gives you new information, highlight it and come back to it. Perhaps make it a point to talk about these meaningful passages with your friends, a therapist, or a coach. When you learn a concept that guides you to think, act, or feel differently, write it on a sticky note and place it in a location that will catch your attention during the day and possibly nudge you in new directions. When you're inspired to deepen your thoughts about your past, present, or future, reconnect with your dreams, or contemplate new possibilities, make the time to explore these thoughts more completely in your journal. Use this book fully. Digest it. Argue with it. Cry with it. Reading it is not enough. Transformation is hard work. It requires your active participation. And, oh yes, the rewards are boundless! Let's get started.

Why Divorce Is So Difficult

Divorce is a traumatic event. It undermines your sense of who you are, your belief about your safety and security, and your understanding about love, family, relationship, commitment, and certainty. The world as you have come to know and live it turns upside down.

To understand this more closely, let's examine what happens within you when you become divorced. Go back to the day of your wedding. What were your thoughts? What were your beliefs about relationships, men, yourself as a partner, marriage, family, and so on? Commonly held beliefs are: "Marriage is forever"; "My marriage vows were sacred"; "Until death us do part"; and "As long we as we both shall live."

Your devotion to these phrases and beliefs began in childhood and, as for most women, became a part of the thoughts that defined your reality as you grew older. Many women grow up imagining a future in which they would be married to one person forever; that they would be honor-bound by their marital vows; and that they would live a life that was, realistically speaking, "happily ever after."

The impact of having to dissolve the images that have been a permanent fixture within and the psychic glue of your entire life may cause you to become disoriented, frightened, lost, and very confused. You may lose your psychological bearings and no longer seem to know who you are, what is important to you, and what you want from life. You are not overreacting to the pain of divorce—it is real and large.

The trauma of divorce has seriously altered many of the fundamental ways that women have been used to thinking about themselves and their lives. This means that it is important to realize that moving ahead will take time and thoughtful rebuilding both inside yourself and in your external, day-to-day life. It will require that you regroup, rethink, and rebuild. This is challenging, yet assuredly possible.

With the new knowledge that divorce is a traumatic event that affects the core of who you are psychologically, comes the realization that rebuilding must also occur at a deep level. Based on well-developed psychology models, you can create a road map to help navigate you through this transformation.

Understanding the Road Ahead

By interacting with this book, you are blazing a new trail as a woman who wants to move beyond her divorce with strength, permanence, and clarity. It's important to be familiar with the teachings of two psychological experts regarding development and transition. The groundbreaking work of Abraham Maslow and William Bridges is strong, initial guidance for your transformational journey ahead.

Maslow's Hierarchy of Needs

Psychologist Abraham Maslow (1987) conceptualized a Hierarchy of Needs, in which he described a progression of basic requirements that humans need to thrive, be productive, and grow psychologically, emotionally, and spiritually. Maslow suggests that as individuals acquire their needs at each level, starting with the most basic, they increase their capacity to achieve more complex degrees of satisfaction in life. Exposure to traumatic events, like divorce, strips away the acquired sense of safety and security, and forces people to return to their most basic needs to rebuild their lives. As you read of Maslow's Hierarchy below, reflect on your experiences. Start with the first moments after you separated from your husband. Notice if your progression of concerns corresponds to the areas in which you were forced to place your attention and energy.

Maslow's Hierarchy of Needs:

Level 1:   Biological, Physical
(Can I provide food, clothing, and shelter for my children and myself?)

Level 2:   Security, Safety
(Am I safe alone? Can I take care of my children and myself?)

Level 3:   Love, Affection, Connection
(Where do I belong? Who cares about me?)

Level 4:   Self-Esteem, Self-Respect, Self-Confidence
(Am I loveable and likeable by others? Do I need a man to be respected by others and myself?)

Level 5:   Growth and Development
(What is important to me? Who do I want to be in this world? In what areas do I want to grow as an adult woman?)

The order of needs and concerns described above provides great direction. It illustrates, one step at a time, one level at a time, areas in which divorced women must thoughtfully place their time and energy in order to move ahead after the trauma of divorce. The first level, for example, biological and physical needs, is a tremendous issue for many newly separated women who are unable to secure an interim agreement with their husbands regarding monetary support.

Frequently, women find themselves stuck at this most basic stage, even after the divorce and a legal agreement is in place. Adjusting to a new style of living, not having enough money to live in the same neighborhood, and coping with the anxiety about future security often stop women from being able to make the adjustment to postmarried life. Women in these predicaments are forced to remain at Maslow's level 1—biological and physical needs—until they find a way to create a sense of security on their own. This is not easy, to be sure, and is an essential building block for transformation.

The chapters that follow will explore new and creative ways to consider dealing with these and other challenges. As you strive to reclaim your life and your sense of self, you will learn the tools needed to transcend any of the levels. Overall, it is essential that you develop an inner tenacity, a stubbornness, about moving up the Hierarchy. A mantra, or repeated phrase, such as "I will not let anything hold me back" internally cheers many women onward. As you attend to your needs, one level at a time, you will step away from your trauma and move closer to living with new possibilities and a vibrant future.

Bridges's Flow of Change

While Maslow teaches about issues that require attention to move confidently ahead, William Bridges, in his books *Transitions* (1980) and *Managing Transitions* (1991), introduces the notion that change is not a singular event, but rather a flow of time whereby you gradually let go of the past and, as you are able, slowly open up to the future.

It is a mistake to think of divorce as a solitary event that happens one day in court. It is far more productive to conceptualize divorce as a passage, a journey, or a transition from what was (marriage) to what will be (your unknown future). During the journey of divorce, you'll travel along a psychological path, moving ahead first as a separated women, and then as a divorced, independent woman. Bridges describes this journey as having three stages, which, if followed gradually and completely, turn major life changes into times of profound growth.

The Endings Phase. Interestingly, Bridges says that the first step of the journey begins with endings. This may strike you as strange at first. Don't new experiences start at the beginning? Bridges doesn't think so: "The new growth cannot take root on ground still covered with the old, and endings are the clearing process" (1980, 91). His description reminded me of my home after my spouse moved out. In the spaces once occupied by his furniture were mounds of dust; in the closet once crowded with his clothes were empty hangers. For there to be room for my things, I needed to clean house. And while I vacuumed and reorganized, I cried.

Endings are excruciating, especially the end of a marriage, which held so many cherished dreams. How do you go on without your dreams? It is very difficult. Abandonment, betrayal, disappointment, powerlessness, rage, all arise during the ending phase. At the bottom of these feelings is fear: How am I going to go on? Will I ever be able to feel joy again? Trust again? Find love again? Want to love again? Be able to love again? Emptiness surrounds you at this ending stage of your transition, which comes largely from a jarring separation from your former identity as part of a family and as part of a couple. When you previously thought of "going home," you knew where you were going and to whom you were going. With that cornerstone missing, along with your dreams, it's easy to feel lost.

Endings are particularly difficult to accomplish if you often have to interact with your former spouse due to shared child custody and financial negotiations. One woman said, "I thought I was doing so well, and then I saw him and broke down all over again." It is a very difficult time, to be sure.

While everyone reacts differently to endings, it is important that you not run from the pain and disorientation or use a lot of external activity to distract you from the internal work you must accomplish. By allowing yourself to be task-oriented and to gradually acclimate to new ways of completing your daily chores (which will include attending to the lower-level needs covered by Maslow), you will accomplish the emotional task of packing up and saying good-bye to the past. Acknowledging the finality of the marriage will allow the seeds of a new future to be planted with no contaminants from the past.

Without clear closure on the past, you will be vulnerable to a future where you may unwittingly repeat your past mistakes or find yourself unable to develop new interests. You may be so consumed by past-oriented resentments and fears that there is no space for any new input. If, however, you allow yourself to journey through your endings by examining what happened, why, and particularly how you might have, perhaps unwittingly, contributed to the separation, then your endings will reward you with a precious and valuable gift—the gift of knowing new, stronger, and wiser ways to create your future.

One of the biggest mistakes that separated and divorced women make is failing to understand that divorce is an ongoing transition, a lengthy journey. They decide one day quite soon after their separation that they are "over their marriage." They buy some new clothes and start making major changes in their lives, typically dating. Clichés that describe this phase include, "Get over it!" and "Don't cry over spilled milk!" These falsely illustrate that the key in life is to put a lid on your past feelings and move ahead. The impulse to follow this guidance often comes from an inability to cope with the emptiness and loneliness of the days and weeks following separation.

While they sipped their afternoon coffee together, Cathy sat with her new acquaintance Bev, who exemplified a rushed and incomplete coping strategy. No matter what Cathy did to steer the conversation in different directions, Bev continually found opportunities to rant and rave about her ex, who she thought was taking unfair advantage of her monetary situation. Needless to say, their time together was very one-sided and not particularly pleasant. Bev had not finalized her feelings about her former spouse (even if that meant begrudgingly accepting her settlement even though she judged it to be unfair), and her negative emotions were leaking into a potential new friendship.

The Endings Phase helps you to think through the past and reformat it so that it becomes a story about a part of your life, not an ongoing reality (hence the phrase "*hi*story," or better still, "*her*story"). The Endings Phase allows you to move ahead unencumbered by the pain, yet knowledgeable about what the past has to teach.

The Neutral Zone: Bridges calls his second stage the Neutral Zone. It is a vulnerable and important time in between what was and what will be: thus the word "neutral." This is a very internally active time that connects the past with the future. It is a time of energetic contemplation, of regrouping, healing, gathering strength, and adjusting to a new way of living. It is a time of great creativity when you can learn from the past and plan for the future. When you are in the Neutral Zone, it may appear to outsiders that you are not doing anything, as you may not be making many external changes in your life. However they would be wrong: you are busy internally preparing a new psychological foundation. If you can continue to tolerate the anxiety of not knowing what is going to happen in your future, which is a very difficult challenge, then the time that you spend in the Neutral Zone will enable you to create a healthy and open space in which the future can take hold. It is normal to feel confused and disorganized during this period of your transition. But from the chaos will come the clarity.

As you walk through the Neutral Zone, your dominant activities will center around laying the groundwork for the future: you will be taking stock of your life; learning new skills; meeting new people; experimenting with new ways to dress, talk, and act; researching new possibilities; and, most of all, reclaiming your dreams and exploring new ways to make them realities. Bridges likens the Neutral Zone to a wilderness. The key is to walk through the wilderness and not to take the beltway around it. The seeds for making your divorce a transformational experience are planted in the Neutral Zone. Future chapters provide you with tools and ideas to help make this time a powerful passage to an exciting future.

Many women jump out of the Neutral Zone too soon. While there is no time requirement for how long to spend here, the first sign that you are ready for the next stage is when you can think of your former spouse, and others associated with your marriage, and you no longer feel a lot of emotional tension. You do not cry; you do not react overtly with anger. You can tell others what occurred and how you felt, and it will feel as though you are telling a story. The events themselves will no longer seem to carry energy with them. You may still be angry or sad, but you can report those feelings objectively and unemotionally as if they were a story about someone else as opposed to expressing them dramatically with tears, rage, and pain.

The Beginnings Stage. Finally, you will make a strong entrance into the final stage of transition, Beginnings. In this stage, you have a clear vision for the future, a well-thought-out strategy that will move you ahead, and a resourceful action plan, including a support system that will help you over the hurdles that you encounter on this last part of the path. The Beginnings Stage will involve creating a new life. You will feel excited, motivated, and resolved to do whatever it takes to move ahead. You'll be at peace knowing that beginnings are not easy, that you will need to expect the unexpected, and that the future will develop slowly, over time, one step after another.

It may be helpful to think of the Beginnings Stage as the *action phase*. It is a time of doing and implementation. Anxiety will come during this phase as you ride the roller coaster of successes and ideas that were great in theory, but did not pan out as you thought they would. There are also "Oh my gosh!" moments when the reality that you are taking independent action, that you are really out there on your own, becomes frightening. What if you fall?

As the name states, the Beginning Stage marks the entrance into your future—it is your beginning. This is an important time to plan celebrations. When you have reached this point in your divorce transition, you will have traveled a long way. Make sure that you take time to be proud of yourself and all of the growing that you have done. This time could also be considered as a kind of birthday. You have given birth to yourself and a new future. It is also helpful to plan times to check in with yourself and others who may be guiding, mentoring, or coaching you. Make sure that you are still on your path, that your expectations are consistent with your initial goals, and that you have the stamina to continue moving ahead.

The Good News and the Challenging News

I remember finishing Bridge's books and releasing a huge sigh of relief at knowing that there was a master plan for moving ahead: that was the good news. I also was uncomfortable that the pain I was feeling would not end quickly over a weekend or with one decision or with one action: that was the challenging news.

Separated or divorced women frequently respond (half) joking to the concept of *Transformational Divorce* by saying: "You mean, a white knight is not going to come and carry me away?" So many separated and divorced women focus on men as the key to a happy future. They are often held back by their own limited visions for what is possible for their futures. Vibrant living requires that you take many steps back and see the rainbow of possibilities that beckon at the horizon, that you throw open your arms and embrace all that your life can be. This can certainly include a loving, deep relationship with a man. The purpose of this book is to encourage you to reclaim more of your dreams than just the one that relates to men. A wonderful future is within your grasp. You are in control of your happily-ever-after.

Finding Your Wants

Divorce is a wake-up call for many women and it can be for you as well. It can help you face the complacency with which you may have been living your life when you were married and challenge you to take charge now by forcing you to grapple with one gigantic question: What do you want?

As a woman, you may have spent so much of your time helping others with their desires that you have little experience focusing on your own. Doris described her first weekend alone without her children as follows:

> The children were with their father. I set as my goal to only engage in those activities that I wanted to do. I sat on my bed stymied. What did I want to do? I decided to start small. I went for a walk. That worked for a while until I grew tired of walking. I heard myself say, "You really should walk a little while longer to receive the best benefits of the exercise." This day was not about "shoulds," it was about "wants." So, realizing that I did not want to walk any

more and that I wanted to go home, I turned around and went home. Now what did I want to do? I wanted to go shopping. So off I went. I stopped after one hour. I didn't want to shop any more. Now what did I want to do? This went on all weekend. It was a lot of work! I learned that I stifled many of my wants by telling myself that what I wanted wasn't realistic, wasn't good for me, or would be judged negatively by others. I learned to put aside what I wanted because others had wants that were more important than mine. I pushed my wants so far away that I felt as though I had no wants at all.

To transform your life and use divorce as a catalyst for growth, you must allow yourself to want and to dream. Dream huge, exciting, expansive dreams. The acknowledgement of your wants and dreams, and your dedication to bringing them into your life, will allow you to leave the past behind and set a course for a new future. Some of your dreams and wants may be able to be satisfied in one afternoon, and some of your dreams may take a lifetime to fulfill. Don't let time scare you. When you see yourself engaging in new activities and walking your journey one small step at a time, that is your evidence that you are growing, changing your life, leaving your divorce behind, and moving into the future. That is transformation.

The Stepping-Stones of Transformation

So how do you start along a new path, strengthen currently problematic areas, and begin to create a wonderful life that reflects your lifelong dreams? One step at a time. While it may be a part of your nature to just dive in and intuitively start to make changes in your life, you may want to try a different approach: contemplate, prepare, act, and keep taking actions toward your dreams (Prochaska, Norcross, and DiClemente 1994). These steps reflect years of research on how people can make long and lasting changes in their lives and enjoy the fruits of their transformations.

Contemplation is critical. It means giving thorough and detailed consideration to all aspects of your life and your dreams. Several of this book's chapters will creatively discuss several key aspects of life so that you can expand your contemplations and really broaden your visions of what your life could look like. After you have thought through your wants and dreams with regards to the different variables of your life, you will be able to *prepare* a plan and then take *action* toward transforming your life. Chapters 8 and 9, respectively, will help you prepare and take continual action so that when you finish this book you will be well on your way toward a vibrant life.

The Pillars of an Independent Woman's Life: A Transformational Exercise

The best way to work toward developing a well-thought-out plan of action is to be clear about where you are right now. The following pillars exercise will help you assess your present satisfaction with the various components of your life, and assist you in beginning to develop visions of your future. You will create the clearest plan if you can take your time and move through the items on the assessment one by one. Assessing and thinking through each exercise component will move you ahead with a sense of clarity, purpose, and direction, and will significantly increase the certainty that the changes you make will be lasting.

Your mission throughout the following exercise is to

♦ take stock of where you are right now,

♦ assess how satisfied you are with different dimensions of your life; and

♦ begin to reclaim your most cherished dreams.

The activity is a modification of the Pillars of Life exercise used and developed by Ben Dean, Ph.D. in his MentorCoach Training Program (2000). Let's get started.

Taking Your First Step

Get a piece of plain white paper. Position it horizontally so that the long side is along the bottom (not the position you typically write in). Draw thirteen long, thin vertical pillars, leaving room at the bottom of the page to label each pillar, and room at the top to write the title of this exercise: "The Pillars of an Independent Woman's Life." Each pillar represents one important facet of your life; a component that contributes to your ability to be a happy, independent, and strong woman. The definition of each of the categories is different for each woman. You can best personalize this exercise by deciding on your own meaning for and description of each topic.

Label the pillars from left to right as follows:

- Home Environment
- Physical Body
- Spiritual Life
- Personal Time
- Financial Wellness
- Family
- Relationship with Former Spouse
- Friends
- Self-Knowledge
- Sense of Independence
- Career/Professional
- Hobbies and Interests
- Intimate Relationships

In each column, record your current level of satisfaction with that specific area of your life on a scale from 1 to 10. Ten would indicate that you could not be happier with the way that you are experiencing that area right now. A score of 1 would mean that you are not pleased with that area right now in any way. When you score a particular area, shade in the portion of the column that reflects your satisfaction from the bottom of the column up. For example, if you score an area as 10, you would fill in the entire column; if you gave the area a 5, you would fill it in halfway, starting from the bottom; a 1 would have little or no filling in the column. This is like a thermometer where no color means no temperature (no satisfaction) and a fully colored thermometer means a lot of fever (lots of satisfaction).

Go through the whole list. Take your time. For each component, close your eyes, go inside yourself, and ask, "How am I doing? How do I feel about this area of my life?" When you have finished, take a break. Self-reflection is draining work.

Congratulations for doing this first exercise; it means that you are taking your transformation very seriously and that you are very committed to making changes that will bring you joy and fulfillment.

Women who take the time to contemplate and plan have the best chance at really impacting their lives. In completing step 1, you have demonstrated your commitment to yourself. This is terrific and very important. Ready to move on?

Taking Your Second Step

Your second task will require that you use your notebook or a journal. This assignment may take some time. It will be most beneficial if you think expansively and thoroughly with this part of the exercise.

For each area listed, describe what a score of 10 would look like. Construct an image of your ideal: if you were really, really happy with each area of your life, what would it look like? What would you be doing? Who would be in your life? What kinds of activities would you be doing? Dare to dream. The more detail you are able to record about your ideals, the more this part of the exercise will serve you later on. Leave plenty of blank space in your journal after you have written about a particular category. You will want to add to your thoughts as you read this book and spend more time thinking and fantasizing about your dreams.

This is an important activity and well worth the investment of your time for several reasons:

1. Recalling your fantasies will give you energy; your dreams are the fuel that drives your actions.

2. Having an image of a 10 will allow you to develop a plan that has a logical series of steps; your plan will move toward a defined outcome.

3. Having a picture of your prize in your mind will motivate you, call you forward, give you something to work toward, and, hopefully, have fun doing it.

Done with step 2? Great! You'll come back to your vision in chapter 6 as you look at ways that you can expand yourself even further and create an almost unthinkable, huge, terrific, audacious, fantastic life vision for yourself. You may begin to identify how you get in your own way and impose limitations on your dreams. This will be addressed later. For now, take a break. Yet, again, you have proven to yourself that you are committed to transforming your life. You have put action behind your wishes. You are on the road!

Your Final Step

It's time to integrate and consider all of the information contained on your Pillars Exercise form. Place your chart in front of you. Notice the scores that reflect how satisfied you are with your life right now. Now, hold an image of your graph in your mind for a moment and recall what you wrote in your notebook or journal about what your life would need to be like for you to rate each category as a 10. Now look back at your chart. The space in each category between your life as it is now and your images of your life with ratings of 10s is the road of your transformation as you embark on a journey toward vibrant living.

A Few Last Questions to Ponder

There are many questions to consider before you actually begin to make significant changes. (Many of them will be addressed throughout the following chapters.) For the moment, however, allow yourself time to ponder, just let your mind wander, and recognize the possibilities that exist if you have the courage to set out toward a new future. Would you have had the freedom and opportunity to make changes in some of these categories while you were still in your marriage? What steps need to be taken so that you can move your life from where you rate it today to a score of 10? Under what conditions would you be willing to take these steps?

At the conclusion of this exercise, many women experience tremendous longing. Some feel they have been so preoccupied with surviving day to day that they have not given much thought to how far away they are from living the life that they have always wanted. They also say that they are enormously pessimistic about their ability to reach a 10 in any category. You may feel similarly. Still, you have a challenge before you to hang in there and navigate through your fears and beliefs about what is and isn't possible. Grab on to your desires to live a fulfilling and happy life. Realize that staying with your unhappy circumstances is no longer acceptable.

As I reflect back during my times of feeling unhappy and stuck, what moved me through those moments was a belief that somewhere there were possibilities that I had yet to consider; that among all of the doors that seemed locked, there was one that was unlocked. My mission was to keep jiggling all of the knobs until I found the open door. I just couldn't stand the powerlessness (and misery) of staying still and not reaching for untried doors. For me, as long as I could discover one more door, there was the possibility that I would not be locked out of the wonderful life that I wanted so badly to live. I invite you to find your unlocked doors.

In the chapters that follow, each of the Pillars of an Independent Woman's Life will be examined. Possibilities and choices that other women have made are available to you, too. You will learn how to plan, how to take action, and how to keep going when success seems to elude you. You will be asked questions and introduced to some concepts that hopefully will open up new ways for you to think about yourself.

As you read this book and actively contemplate your life that was and your life that can be, remember that underneath any fear that you may feel is a rich storehouse of strength, potential, and talent. The trauma that occurs with divorce may interfere with your ability to feel confident and capable, wise and knowing, but your riches are there nonetheless. As you begin to make some changes, no matter how small they may seem compared to the size of your dreams, an increased sense of confidence will follow. It will grow and expand as your transformation unfolds. There is no end to what you can accomplish.

Chapter 2

Building a Strong Foundation

Women embrace the change that accompanies separation and divorce in many different ways. None of the styles is right or wrong; each has its challenges and benefits. The key is identifying your "way," accepting it even if you see another woman behaving differently, and then allowing your transformation to unfold according to the rhythms and energies within you.

Are You a Jumper or a Ponderer?

There are two common themes to how women handle change. Which personality best describes you: a *jumper* or a *ponderer?* Knowing your tendencies will enable you to capitalize on your strengths and help you to work with those parts of yourself that feel more stubborn and resistant to taking those next important steps toward your future dreams.

Although there are two types of personalities that describe divorced women on the brink of their journeys into the future, you will probably see yourself possessing elements of both descriptions. This is to be expected; however, you may find yourself more like one than another, or prone to acting one way in a given situation and another way in a different set of circumstances. Read the descriptions below and see what you can learn about yourself. It might help if you take a highlighter and color the characteristics of each type that seem to describe you. Later you can review what you noted was familiar and reflect further on your type.

Jumpers

Jumpers are typically excited about change and want to make it happen immediately. They may be eager because they are optimistic about their futures or because they have been taught "Don't cry over spilled milk" and are anxious to "get on with it." Jumpers either do not want to do a lot of self-reflection or they feel more comfortable putting aside thinking about the past, their psychological growth, or their visions of the future until after their immediate world (for example, their home, schedule, or financial life) is more settled and predictable. Jumpers have the energy necessary to begin transforming their environment and circumstances soon after their relationship is finished. This fast response allows them to create a momentum for change that typically feels positive and sets the stage for more changes to occur—change begets more change.

The warning for Jumpers is that sometimes their changes can be shallow. Jumpers can get so engaged in making external modifications to their lives, such as to their home, social life, or body, that they fail to attend to the transformations that are happening inside of themselves. They don't ask questions such as "Who am I?" or "Who do I see myself becoming in the future?" "What is important to me?" "What do I really value?" Without this introspection they may find themselves quickly outgrowing, disliking, or unable to sustain the changes that they have made. Another problem with being a Jumper is that they often feel as if they are riding an emotional roller coaster. They try one activity, are excited about it's potential, and then, if it doesn't bring the imagined results, they feel disappointed. Then they try something else, get excited about that, and so forth. Jumpers thrive on activity and being busy. When there is a lull in their schedule, Jumpers may find themselves sad or depressed.

In summary, Jumpers are action-oriented changers who are able to engage quickly in the process of transformation. Their challenge is to blend their strengths—energy and the ability to take risks—with introspection, an activity in which they often do not give themselves time to engage.

Ponderers

Ponderers are slower to initiate and embrace change than Jumpers. Ponderers are thinkers, contemplators, and planners. They place a great deal of importance on understanding their circumstances—past, present, and future—and want to make sure that their actions are well conceived and thought through. Ponderers may either be thorough, wanting to make changes only when they know that they have learned all they need to learn before acting, or cautious and timid, being fearful of moving ahead due to the potential of disappointment and pain.

Ponderers tend to give themselves time to grow into their transformations; they integrate what they have learned from their experiences, and their slow and steady pace contributes strength to their transformational process. The change momentum for Ponderers, however, can easily become stalled. They may struggle with their energy levels to the point of not being able to make change happen—inaction produces inaction. It is critical that Ponderers be clear as to whether they are truly contemplating their circumstances to plan or better understand, or whether they are avoiding making external changes in their life because they are afraid of the future, afraid of letting go of the past, afraid of taking risks, or a bit of all of the above.

In summary, Ponderers are internally oriented changers whose focus of transformation is on understanding where they were, where they are now, and where they are headed in the future. Their challenge is to blend their strength—their solid understanding of themselves and their circumstances—with the energy and courage necessary to bring about tangible changes in their day-to-day life.

Blending the Styles

Learn to be both a Ponderer and a Jumper. When you find yourself behaving in one mode, make sure you take some time to balance it with activities from the other mode. If you find that you have been jumping and energetically engaging in many activities, stop, take out your journal, and ponder. How does this new direction feel? While you may be feeling excited, is there a part of you that is also feeling frightened? Have you thought through the actions that you are about to take? How will the changes fit into your life in the future? If the actions do not promote the change that you were anticipating, what will you do? How will you feel? Do you have a contingency plan or an alternative plan?

If you find that your predominant activities are reading, thinking, therapy, journaling, or introspection, challenge yourself by asking, "Am I avoiding moving ahead?" "Is there some, maybe small, action that I feel comfortable taking at this time?" "Is my 'pondering' actually moving me forward or keeping me back?"

Action combined with contemplation is the key to transformation. Utilizing the strengths of each personality type—the energetic risk-taking spirit of the Jumper *and* the quiet, thorough introspective nature of the Ponderer—will enable you to initiate and maintain a transformation that has creativity and depth.

Five Foundations of Transformation

To be a woman is to have a broad range of interests, needs, and responsibilities. To survive, you must attend to the "basic necessities": food, clothing, and shelter, and a minimal amount of money to purchase items to sustain you. To move into your future with strength, clarity, and purpose, however, it is also essential that you attend to parts of yourself that you may not usually include on your list of "necessities": your physical being, your spiritual needs, and time to yourself. Focusing on these components will help you bring balance to the multiple roles that compete for your energy. At the beginning stages of your transformation, focus on five foundational elements of your life: home environment, physical body, spiritual life, personal time, and financial wellness. As you feel that you are gaining control over these areas and that each area has the potential to grow, develop, and reflect your capacity for depth and joy, then the foundation will truly be laid for an animated, expansive future.

Creating Your Home Environment

Begin laying the foundation of transformation with creating a home of your own. Claiming the space where you live, sleep, raise your children, and retreat is probably the most foundational aspect of your life, even though in some ways, many take this space for granted. When you are separated or divorced, the home becomes a focal point for many struggles and often seems to be the stage on which many women feel the intense emotions of being on their own. Because the home can be a venue for complications and pain, it is very important to work vigorously to transform it into a space in which you feel safe and nurtured. Claiming your home as your own can also be a fun and playful process where you can let your imagination run wild by expressing yourself with colors, textures, and favorite objects. Approach with open arms the project of claiming your home. Realize that because this space is yours, you can do anything that you *want* with it. There's that word "want" again. As was discussed in chapter 1, it may take you some time to embrace in an expansive way—or even to know—what you want, especially you Ponderers. That's OK, there is a viable path of transformation for everyone. Remember, transformation has nothing to do with time and speed—it's about movement, one step at a time.

Home Space and Limitations

It is impossible to approach the topic of home without recognizing the many limitations that women face in this area. Divorce necessitates that many women leave their homes and move into quarters that are smaller, less desirable, and in neighborhoods that are less costly. The economics of divorce often require that women move in with their parents or other family members. Turning challenges into opportunities is an important shift in attitude. The following pages contain different ways to optimize housing comprimises.

A Model to Consider

In the early 1980s, there was a television show called *Kate and Allie*, which depicted two divorced, thirty-something mothers who decided to combine their households and live together. The show was funny and touching as it followed the situations that these two women faced raising their children together, pooling their economic resources, babysitting for each other so that each could begin dating, and so forth.

The *Kate and Ally* model is a viable and creative paradigm that could be considered by some divorced women as a potential solution to postdivorce living and logistical difficulties. Of course, any time two adults live together there are interpersonal complications to be faced as well as financial and organizational issues, but most of these are resolvable. The next chapter will explore more about the importance of ongoing connections and how divorced women can prosper significantly through the development of community in its many forms. For the purposes of this chapter, however, the idea of combining households is an alternative for women and their families, especially when confronted with economic difficulties. The key to transformation is searching for possibilities, for solutions to the difficulties that confront you, and refusing to be stuck because of your circumstances. As you face the importance of creating your space, exploring different options is important.

The Disappointment of Having to Move

One of the most difficult parts of the divorce process is coping with the sense that you're moving backward with respect to standard of living, particularly when it means selling a home that you love or having to share a room with your child. Do everything in your power to resist becoming a hostage to disappointments, anger, and sadness. While it is understandable that you would prefer to live in your former, perhaps larger, home, your anger at the situation will block you from creating a situation in the present that will sustain you in the here and now, and help you to develop the energy and drive that you need to create a new terrific future in a new home that is totally yours.

Journey to Your Space: A Transformational Exercise

Take out your Pillars Exercise form. On the column labeled "Home Environment" how did you rate your satisfaction in this area? Take some time to write down in detail why you rated it as you did.

Nancy shared the following: "I rated my home a 3. My husband moved out about two months ago. He took his clothes with him, but everything else is still here. It is impossible to think of this space as 'mine' as his stuff is still all over the house. Also, I am not a great housekeeper and the place, to be honest, is a mess. Although my home should be a nurturing place, well, it really isn't. It is just the place I come to at the end of the day. I don't have the money to fix it up and I don't even know if we are going to stay here."

What do you think of Nancy's response? Many women get stuck in that in between time when "his stuff" is still there. It really does interfere with the ability to experience the home as your own. Also interesting are Nancy's comments that her home felt messy and not nurturing, just functional, and that she felt constrained by her lack of funds and the possibility that this house would not be the place in which she would live long term. Does any of this sound familiar to you?

Take a moment and reflect on what you wrote during the "10" part of the Pillars Exercise. When you described your ideal home, what did you write? Feel free to elaborate on your response right now. The more extensive your response, the more information you will have to develop a plan that really fulfills your desires.

With your current rating as a starting point, and your ideal as a beacon for your dreams, the transformation process can begin. Start with this question: If you were to change your current situation very slightly so that you could rate it a half a step higher (such as from 3.0 to 3.5) what alteration would you make? In other words, what could you do to your home environment that would allow you to enjoy it a bit more? When Nancy answered this question she responded, "I can't begin to enjoy this house with his stuff all over it." She began her transformational journey by gathering together all of his possessions and putting them in the basement. What do you need to do to start enjoying your home?

A Place to Begin

When I began to transform my home, friends helped to make the initial step special. The first place in my house that I wanted to claim absolutely as my own was my bedroom. Many women enjoy starting here as it represents a space that was once shared in a very intimate way. I envisioned creating a beautiful, feminine Victorian-type bedroom that was lavender and white. I bought several magazines that helped me put images to my concept. I wanted a new bed. I began to put money aside each month to purchase the dream bed that I had found in a store catalog; however, I didn't want to wait to purchase the bed to begin the transformation. One friend came to the rescue and took me shopping at a department store during a white sale. She introduced me to thread counts (the number indicates the softness of sheets) and duvet covers, and showed me pillows that could give my room a sense of softness and creativity. One item at a time, I gradually brought objects to my new space. People started to give me purple trinkets and sweet-smelling bath products. I called my bedroom "a work in progress." It took quite a while to complete my vision. The addition of each article, however, made me feel that I was doing something really wonderful for myself. My bedroom became a safe and nurturing haven: a place where I could close the door and concentrate on what was important to me.

Tangible Suggestions

You, too, can claim special places in your home. Here is a list of ideas that other women have tried:

♦ Put new sheets on the bed as soon as he leaves.

♦ Move all of his possessions to one room and close the door. Once the divorce is final, give him one month to clear the room out. When the month passes, give his things to charity.

♦ Plant a garden with beautiful flowers.

♦ If your space is small, claim a corner of the house exclusively as yours; put a chair and small shelf or table there so that you can sit and enjoy yourself and special items.

♦ Keeping the house neat and clean (or just the space that you use often) is a way to honor yourself.

♦ Buy scented candles, spray, or incense, so that your space smells nice.

♦ Spread blank paper on the walls and fill it with your favorite images from magazines.

♦ If you can't afford a nice dining room table, get an old one from a yard sale and cover it with a pretty sheet.

♦ Decorate your space with favorite toys from childhood. Buy yourself a new toy from time to time.

♦ Place pictures of your friends and favorite people all over your home.

♦ Read decorating magazines in the library to learn inexpensive ways to personalize small and large spaces.

The key to making space yours is personalization, allowing your home or any space in which you live to reflect the most life-loving parts of you. Whether you own a large home or share a place with someone else, make sure that you have some space that is absolutely yours—even one shelf—and use it as a launching pad from which more transformation will flow.

Transforming and Claiming Your Body

Women's relationships with their bodies are often geared around what attracts men or pleases the men with whom they are connected. One of the many gifts of divorce is that it forces you to become clear as to what is important to you and to you alone. What relationship do you want to have with your body? This is not an easy question as, from a very early age, your body has been a topic of public discussion and judgments: in the media (beauty pageants and fashion magazines); among female friends ("Sally seems to have put on a few pounds, don't you think?"); in your family of origin ("Honey, don't you think your hair is a bit too long?"); and in your marriage, where you may have dressed and altered your body to please your husband. It's shocking that women speak more often about the look of their bodies than about keeping their bodies healthy. How you view your physical body and health is the second foundational area of transformation. Take some time now to consider the way that you think about your body.

Physical Health

How much do you think about your short-term and long-term physical health? Do you go for a yearly physical examination? Do your eating and exercise habits reflect love for yourself? According to life-stress scales, divorce ranks among the top most stressful events that you can experience. This means that you have an increased chance of illness, exhaustion, and depleting your body's resources during this very painful time.

For transformation to occur, for you to have the energy and strength that you need to move into your future, you need to take care of your body. Not only is health care an important physiological activity, but when you engage in behaviors that nurture, protect, and sustain your most basic self, you send a message to your psyche that says, "I am important." This powerful communication becomes a foundation for other actions that you take. You're able to develop the psychic and physical energy that you need to be creative, to successfully move through the barriers that inevitably block your journey, and to sprint toward your goals with vitality and exuberance. Women generally are "other focused." That is, you may take care of everyone else, all other jobs and responsibilities, before attending to yourself. Do as flight attendants suggest in airplanes: "First place the oxygen mask over your own mouth, and then help those around you."

Self-Care: A Transformational Exercise

If physical self-care is an area that you tend to ignore, one that you rated with lower numbers on your Pillars Exercise, consider raising your score with actions that you can easily accomplish. For example, drink more water each day—even one more glass—or park a few feet further away from the stores when you need to do an errand so that you can take some extra steps. As you feel more energetic, consider making an appointment for a physical examination, as well as dental and eye examinations.

Women's health is now receiving more attention from the medical community, and more books are being published on topics such as menopause, aging, exercise, and skin care. Knowing more about the needs of your body will help you to design your transformational vision in this area. Choose your starting place. You will be immediately rewarded with waves of positive energy. Before reading further, write in your journal three to five ways that you can begin right now. A commitment to your health paves the way for healthy commitments in other areas.

Physical Appearance

There are few areas in which women are as influenced by the opinions and values of others as they are about their physical appearance, their outer beauty. Again, here is a part of your life in which you must decide what is important to you, and to you alone. Two realities affect this area:

1. When you have positive feelings about your outer appearance, you tend to feel more positively about yourself.

2. Elements of your outer appearance impact the responses you receive from others.

Therefore, making decisions about your outer appearance is another component of taking charge of your life. What is your philosophy about physical beauty and the outer image you want to portray?

Physical Evolution: A Transformational Exercise

Return to the Pillars Exercise and begin to map out a course for transforming your physical self. It might be helpful to subdivide the Physical Pillar into two categories: health and outer appearance. Divide both categories even further so that they best reflect areas that are important to you. For example, you might include eating, exercise, self-care, clothes, makeup, skin, and hair. Keep a list of all subcategories. In chapters 6, 8, and 9, which address developing a vision, a plan, and taking action, you will come back to this list and integrate all of your directions into a coherent plan for transformation. For now, however, think about your current level of satisfaction in the physical arena. How happy are you right now with this component of your life? If you were to increase your level of satisfaction by just a half a point, say from 3.0 to 3.5, what would you change?

Here are some ideas that other women have pursued:

♦ Hire a personal trainer, purchase an exercise video, or commit to watching an exercise program on television.

♦ Receive a full physical checkup, including mammogram, dental check, and eye exam.

♦ Visit department stores and try on new clothes.

♦ Collect pictures from magazines of your "ideal look."

♦ Experiment with a new hairstyle or color.

♦ Get a tattoo.

♦ Receive a free makeover at the cosmetics counter.

♦ Drink more water daily.

♦ Join a weight-loss program.

♦ Read a book on healthy eating.

♦ Visit a nutritionist.

♦ Quit smoking, drinking, or eating sugar.

♦ Find a walking buddy to walk with three times per week.

The possibilities are limited only by your creativity. Above all, make sure that your decisions match your values, and avoid doing what you think you "should." Engage only in those actions you feel ready to integrate into your life on an ongoing basis. Experiment at first. Find your look, your way, your values. Your body is about you. Divorce brings into sharp focus the reality that you are individually responsible for all of the aspects of your life, especially with regard to your health, well-being, and sense of external beauty. Your body is the vessel for your heart and spirit. During this time of being fully independent, you can transform your body, the physical container of all that you are, so that it expresses the essence within you.

Beginning Your Spiritual Transformation

A third foundational area of transformation is your spiritual life. The word *spiritual* has different meanings, the common denominator of which is the function that it plays in your life. "Spiritual" is often used to describe the collection of beliefs that make sense of people's existence. Spirituality can call you inward to a personal and quiet space and help you to feel settled during challenging times, such as divorce, when you are juggling many changes. Once you have found your spiritual core, you will have a major piece of strength that will support you on the more difficult parts of your transformational journey. When actions feel impossible, and hope is lost, some form of spiritual belief or practice can provide a lifeline connecting you to the more resilient parts of yourself that know how to survive and move forward.

For many women, life on their own, without a man, provides an opening to explore a kind of spirituality that didn't seem available before. In a desire to connect deeply with your spouse, you may have compromised your own practices or beliefs. You may have attended church or synagogue less than you would have liked; or you may not have read about new spiritual ideas in fear that you would be judged. Being on your own creates privacy to consider and try both new and traditional forms of spirituality. Here, you may find hope, solace, and connection.

Spiritual transformation is a wonderfully expansive journey where you become attuned to new questions about your past, present, and future. You can search for ways to understand your relationships and the people in your life. You can utilize a perspective that places life in the context of something much larger than day-to-day existence.

When a woman begins to transform her spiritual world and learn new ways to think about herself, she is able to make profound changes in how she sees herself, the choices that are available to her, and the impact that she can have on her life. She becomes empowered. By attending to her essential self—the part of her that exists outside of her tasks, her roles, and her relationships—she is able to see herself in a new light and deep change can happen.

One woman described her spiritual journey as "magic." She said, "Once I started reading, meditating, walking, and being open to learning from everyone and every experience, all the pieces of my life began to fall into place." This woman found the power to be fully herself, a capacity that had been locked up within her since the day she was born. Divorce and spirituality had unlocked the gate, and she was now able to experience her life and the world around her in new ways.

A full discussion about spirituality is beyond the scope of this book. There are hundreds of wonderful authors who have shared spiritual concepts and practices more fully. The focus here is to find ways to begin to utilize divorce as an opening to explore all avenues of your life, including the importance of the spiritual. If you can see your divorce as both a crisis and an opportunity (a philosophy expounded in Chinese spirituality), then you are well on the way toward claiming the full potential of your life. Your spiritual transformation has begun.

Inviting the Spiritual: A Transformational Exercise

Return to the Pillars Exercise and look at the satisfaction rating that you placed on your Spiritual Pillar. How happy are you right now with the role that spirituality has in your life? What is happening in your spiritual life that causes you to rate spirituality in this way? After answering these questions in your journal, choose one small activity that will enhance your experience with spirituality. What could you do in the next few days that will allow you to feel calmer, perhaps learn a new concept, or connect to spirituality in a way that you have not done for a while or maybe even ever?

Here is a list of activities that some women have found helpful:

- ◆ Visit different churches or synagogues.
- ◆ Read books on spirituality.
- ◆ Meditate or take a meditation class.
- ◆ Attend workshops.
- ◆ Create a "spiritual space" in your home for special objects.
- ◆ Light candles.
- ◆ Pray.
- ◆ Join a women's spirituality group.
- ◆ Talk to ministers, rabbis, or chaplains.
- ◆ Write in your journal.

- ◆ Contemplate the meaning of forgiveness and letting go.

- ◆ Become involved in volunteer work.

- ◆ Talk to other women about their spiritual practices and beliefs.

As you have done in other areas, consider choosing one activity and allow yourself to experiment. What would it be like to expand the way you experience yourself as a spiritual woman? Note the impact that this has on the way you feel about yourself and your life.

Transforming Personal Time and Financial Wellness

Divorced women often state that limitations of time or money keep them from transforming the other three foundational areas (home, physical self, and spiritual life). The key to pushing forward is identifying and creating choices rather than feeling helpless and stuck. When you look at the world in terms of available choices as opposed to overwhelming limitations, you are powerful instead of powerless.

Dancing between Powerful and Powerless

Women often speak about feeling powerless, that they have little control over the circumstances that happen to them. There is a significant reality to this perception: your postmarital finances are determined by legal agreements; your ability to purchase necessities is determined by the amount of money that you can earn; your capacity to give birth is determined by the condition of your body; your economic advancement is determined by your bosses; and so on. In many ways, circumstances and other people control some of life's most important directions.

To reclaim your sense of power, it is important that you transform this barrier into a challenge. What if you stopped focusing on the courses of action that are not available to you, and instead focused on the circumstances that are within your control? How would your life be different if you emphasized your reactions, your responses, and your options instead of the movements and decisions of others?

As a divorced woman, you will often walk the line between powerfulness and powerlessness. Your true power begins the moment you choose to find the possibilities and reject the notion that you are a victim. Several times a day, say to yourself, "As a powerful woman, I will turn my dreams into my reality."

Becoming Powerful. To expand your sense of power regarding time and money, ask yourself these two questions:

1. Is there any place where I can cut back and redirect my expenditure of time or money?

2. What can I do that will create more time or money?

Try approaching these questions with a completely open mind. Do not get blinded by assumptions or your usual way of experiencing time and money. Try *thinking upside down*. That is, turn your perspectives upside down. If you can view your use of time and money in a new way, all kinds of choices will become apparent.

Expenditures: A Transformational Exercise

To flush out choices about how you spend your personal time and financial wellness, try this exercise. Take out two pieces of paper and do the identical process for both time and money.

On the top of one piece of paper write, "Personal Time." Across the top of the second piece write, "Financial Wellness." Divide both papers into three vertical columns. Label the first column on each paper "Expenditures," the second column "Questions," and the third column "Actions." In column 1, do two things: First make a list of all of the required ways in which you spend time and money. Your list of time requirements may include sleep, work, preparing for work, or helping your children in the morning. In the money area, your list will probably include taxes, housing, insurance, utilities, and food. It may also include items on which you owe money, such as a car payment or credit card debt.

Next, in the same column 1, write down the items or circumstances that are optional, that is, where you have some choice as to whether and how much time or money to spend. Often choices can feel like requirements because they are very important to you, such as private school for your children or areas of personal care. In reality, however, they are choices, as they are not absolute requirements—there are no legal or survival ramifications if you don't spend your time or money on them.

In column 2, "Questions," refer to each expenditure that you listed in column 1. For each item, write a question that asks if there is another way that you could fulfill the obligation so that you could pay less. For example, you might ask, "Is there a way that I could lower my taxes?" "Is there a way that I could pay less rent or mortgage?" "Is there a way that I could feel comfortable with less sleep?" or "Is there a way that I could take less time getting ready in the morning?"

In column 3, "Action," write several ideas that can help you answer your question. Fight off the impulse to immediately answer your question with, "No!" The act of inquiry creates the possibility that your actions can take a new, more favorable form. This allows you to have the potential of changing your circumstances and you become powerful. For example, under taxes you might write, "Consult a tax accountant and see if I am claiming the right amount of deductions." For the question, "Could I pay less money for utilities?" you might write, "Consult electric company and see if they have a budget plan" or "Research ways that I could cut my use of electricity."

For optional expenditures, ask yourself how your life would be different if you did without this item, or ask if there is a way that you can do with less, such as take less time or spend less money. Push yourself to generate ideas that might seem ridiculous at first. Ask your friends, your therapist, family members, or your coach to help you brainstorm ideas. Do not reject the idea of asking people and organizations for help.

For example, when Leslie wanted to visit her son at college, the hotel close to his school was very expensive. She called the manager of the hotel, told him that she was a single mother visiting her son, and asked if he would give her a lower rate. He cut the rate in half! Leslie didn't have to ask for charity or describe herself as a hardship case. She simply told him that she wanted to stay in his hotel and that the price was more than her budget could allow. She was powerful. She was able to impact her budget. If you are able to alter the way that you spend money by only a few dollars per month, you will have begun the process of transformation in this important area.

Creating Time and Money: A Transformational Exercise

The previous exercise focused on changing what you currently have and how you behave with respect to personal time and financial wellness. By looking at your situation again, in a different, more expansive way, you may find some ways to increase what you have while using relatively little effort.

Active, creative, open-minded brainstorming will help you push beyond the limits of your current imagination. *Brainstorming* is the act of quickly thinking up many ideas, one after another, without evaluating them. Many people use the word brainstorming, but few people really fully engage in it. They think too much and stop themselves from saying really big ideas that feel strange or unbelievable.

Take out two more pieces of paper. Label one "Personal Time," and the other "Financial Wellness." Open your brain very wide and allow your thoughts and ideas to pour onto the papers. To engage in this exercise, turn off any part of your personality that tends to be skeptical, judgmental, pessimistic, or negative. To receive the full benefits of brainstorming you need to be open, a little bit wild and crazy, energetic, and creative. Ready?

For personal time and then for money, take ten minutes each and brainstorm answers to this question: "If I could keep my life basically as it is right now, and add activities that will bring more personal time (or money) into my life, would could I do?" The quantity of time or money that your idea could generate doesn't matter. Do not allow yourself to stop writing and brainstorming for ten minutes. Let your imagination soar. The more ideas, the better you're doing. Don't worry if your ideas are realistic. If you find yourself saying, "I can't do that because. . . ," write the thought down anyway. You'll deal with reality later. For now, let go and brainstorm.

You should have on your papers about twenty ideas each for time and money. Your job now is to see if you can find a way to use each of your ideas. Imagine that every concept you brainstormed came from somewhere deep inside of you. This part of you has great wisdom. Your job is to find a piece of each idea, no matter how small, that may be useable at some time. Some thoughts may not be viable, but could lead you to a different, more feasible idea. You don't have to act on anything yet. Right now you are contemplating potential.

To increase your sense of power, it helps to have an *idea list* to which you can refer when you have the time or energy to take a new action. You might not choose to use one of your ideas for a year or two. That's fine. Keep it on your list.

Here are ideas that other divorced women developed when they brainstormed:

- Baby-sit one weekend per month.

- Have a huge yard sale.

- Wake up fifteen minutes earlier.

- Contact and occasionally work for a catering company.

- Implement a strict bedtime for the children.

- Read a book while walking on the treadmill.

- Put a pad of paper in the car to generate ideas.

- Take a bartending course.

- Move to an area where the cost of living is less.

- Trade chores or baby-sitting with another parent.

- Form a cooking cooperative for meals.

- Join a buying cooperative and purchase items in bulk.

Look for the "Yes!" within you. The word "no" blocks you from moving ahead. The "Yes!" is a solution to a problem to which you can say, "Yes, I can do that." Maybe you don't want to baby-sit for an entire weekend, but you could say "Yes!" to one evening. Transformation requires letting go of old solutions and trying new ones. They may not work at first or at all, but the acts of trying and doing are important. By saying "Yes!" you are refusing to stay stuck and powerless, and reaching to change your life.

Returning to the Pillars Exercise

With a new sense of power, return to the Personal Time and Financial Wellness sections of the Pillars Exercise. Reflect on the actions that you listed in the previous exercise. Choose one task to do in the next few weeks that will elevate your time or money rating one half of a point (for example, from 3.0 to 3.5). In attending to your wants, you are becoming powerful. You are effecting your transformation.

Reflections on Creating Your Foundation

Transformation in the areas of home environment, your body, spiritual life, personal time, and financial wellness, lay the groundwork for growth. As you begin to alter these areas to reflect your style, character, needs, and personality, you will feel more settled and soon gain the confidence that you need to venture outside of your comfort zone and engage with people and ideas that are new. Divorce has shaken up your world. Transformation of your foundational areas allows you to settle and become grounded again.

Chapter 3

Connecting with Women Friends

Connection forms the foundation of a woman's psyche and spirit. Women thrive when they are in connection with other women. Almost every divorced and divorcing woman says that her relationships with new women friends helps make the transition of divorce survivable, transformational, and even great fun. Despite the importance and growth potential of female friendships, many women dismiss the idea of meeting and developing closer friendships with other women. They say that they don't enjoy spending time with women and that it's not a priority.

Perhaps the rejection of making new women friends comes from a history of unsatisfying and often traumatizing relationships with females, particularly during adolescence. Teenage issues of competition, jealousy, needs for attention and affirmation, and the like, often contaminate the potential treasures of adult friendships. To transform this important and healing area of your life, try to put the past aside and take a fresh look at the potential of having female friends: shared resources, support, companionship, encouragement, fun, compassion, a sense of belonging, and more. Even the process of getting to know a new female friend will give you the opportunity to expand your interpersonal skills, which benefits your relationships with colleagues, family, and men.

The popular book *Circle of Stones* suggests that women should reach beyond the discomfort of their pasts to explore the kind of intimacy that is possible in female friendships. "How might your life have been different, if, through the years, there had been a place where you could go? . . . A place of women, away from the ordinary busy-ness of life . . . a place of women who knew the cycles of life, the ebb and flow of nature, who knew of times of work and times of quiet . . . who understood your tiredness and need for rest. . . . How might your life be different?" (Duerk 1990, 60).

The aim of this chapter is to inspire and guide you to develop your own circle of female support, compassion, and strength. Close, meaningful relationships with women boundlessly multiply your ability to transform life.

Female Connection Is Empowering

Many women misinterpret the pain of loneliness and isolation that often accompanies divorce as meaning that they are not likeable. This misconception seems to weigh down divorce recovery more than any other single factor. The experience of meeting new friends is often the catalyst that brings about larger changes. Women become more active, adventurous, and empowered; and, if they haven't been able to before, begin to believe that they can survive the challenges that lie ahead. Although bouts of feeling alone occasionally occur, the time spent with women friends and acquaintances provides energizing resources for support, laughter, and probing the depths of possible, positive change.

Women increase one another's capacity to handle various challenges. The day-to-day problems of living are explained, such as ways to fix the disposal or how cut the lawn; psychological quandaries are resolved, such as coping with anger or developing the courage to try something new; resources are shared, such as shelter, food, child care, information, and transportation; holidays and celebrations, which are often lonely for divorced women, are reclaimed and become more fun than ever before.

Women magnify one another's sense of power and ability. One group of women friends, for example, purchased an elaborately designed necklace that they give each week to the woman in greatest need of support. "When I wear it, it's as if I have the strength of each woman embracing me. There is nothing that I can't say or do," one woman explained. The consistency of connection and the resilient spirit these women have developed by gathering each week has enabled each to create a life that none were able to imagine before meeting one another.

Women are able to create more powerful and extensive life transformations when they have a network of friends and connections versus when they live in relative isolation. If your last experience of being a part of an active social group was during high school, becoming ready to actively connect with many different women most likely requires that you alter how you think about friendships in general.

An Expanded Model

When you were younger, perhaps in high school, your best friend most likely occupied a very sacred place in your heart: she was the one with whom you most enjoyed doing activities, shared your most confidential secrets, and occupied most, if not all, of your time talking on the telephone. During the teenage years, best friends use phrases such as "Me too" or "I feel the same way." In mirroring each other's emotions and opinions, best friends helped each other to know and connect with themselves a bit better.

Adults, however, outgrow the need for only one close friend. As intellectual capacity expands with age to incorporate many experiences, ideas, and people, so does the desire to have many friends that can relate in different ways.

Shifting your focus in relationships from a best friend to a network of friends requires that you develop a different intention when seeking companionship. As a teenager, you may have been satisfied with one person, or a small group (a clique) that possessed a set of very similar characteristics. As an adult woman, the search for friendship must be broader and reflect the more complex being that you have become.

Women often find other women with whom they share interests, such as tennis or hiking, but sometimes these individuals lack other qualities that would make them good friends. Rejecting an individual because she cannot fulfill all of your needs is an example of relying on adolescent conceptualizations of friendship. A more mature model allows for different gradations of relationships. Where it was less possible to converse with someone outside of your peer group when you were younger, it is now possible to develop a pool of friends about whom you have an array of feelings.

For example, you might feel comfortable having coffee and talking about children with a mother from your children's school, but not feel open to discussing issues related to your divorce. On the other hand, you may find a woman who elicits your absolute trust and in whom you can confide your fears and vulnerabilities, yet she isn't a person with whom you would enjoy having a playful, mindless weekend at the beach. It is important to identify women who relate to all the different parts of your being—one person does not have to meet all of your needs to be a friend.

Try conceptualizing your friendships as a series of concentric circles, like a dartboard. Ten is the circle on the outer rim; one is the innermost circle, which represents your most intimate connection, namely your relationship with yourself. At this point, you and only you are aware of your secrets, your longings, and your truth. Each circle away from this center point encompasses connections in which you are less open about the personal and private aspects of your life.

Most adolescent girls conceptualize their friendships as occupying the innermost rungs of their charts. They typically reject peers with whom they share lesser levels of intimacy. As an adult woman, however, you have the intellectual ability to understand the complexities of your feelings and connections. You relate to many different people and create relationships in which you enjoy varying levels of closeness (placed at varying points on your friendship chart).

The purpose of this conceptualization is to validate all of the relationships in your life—they all have a very important function as they provide unique levels of companionship. None should be discarded or considered nonessential. One recently divorced woman, Jill, frequently feels uncomfortable with her neighbors, with whom she believes she has little in common. At first, Jill wondered whether she should move and find a community where there were women to whom she could feel closer. When she learned to enjoy the neighborhood women as level 6, 7, and 8 relationships, it allowed her to include them in her life without being disappointed that they aren't the bosom buddies she has always hoped to have as friends. At the same time, she continues looking for women with whom she might have more in common and be able to establish level 3, 4, and 5 relationships.

Legitimize your relationships with women. Do not dismiss them if they are not the kind of friend you would like them to be. Who knows, maybe, over time, the relationship will naturally move to a closer or more remote circle on your chart.

The Nature of Your Female Relationships

What kinds of female relationships are filling your life right now? Knowing the answer to this question will help you devise a plan to transform your social life. Have you have brought people into your life who provide you with the support and enjoyment that you want and need?

A Connections Chart: A Transformational Exercise

Draw a large circle in your journal. Inside of this circle, make nine gradually smaller, concentric circles. For each woman who currently is in your life, make a mark on the chart according to how close you feel to her. Just as before, the outer rim of the circle is level 10, the innermost circle is level 1. Your more intimate friends will have marks closer to the center of this chart. Try to account for all the women you have some sort of connection with, even those with whom you rarely communicate. The more relationships you include in this exercise, the more profound will be the feedback that you receive when you are finished.

Now take a step back and look at your Connections Chart. Do you have relationships spread among most of the different circles? If they tend to cluster in the outer rings, you might want to ask yourself why. Reject the thought that there are no women in your locale with whom you can make a meaningful connection. Instead, use the data in this exercise as motivation for transformation. How might you change yourself or your involvement in activities so that you can have more connections with various kinds of women? What can you do differently to build a network of friends who make useful contributions to your life? Having the courage to ask yourself these difficult questions will open the door to the potential for exciting growth.

Where can you find women friends? Anywhere you allow yourself to engage in a conversation with a woman who seems interesting to you. You might find new acquaintances browsing in your favorite bookstore, on a spiritual retreat, during a walk around the neighborhood, at a lecture on astronomy, at a PTA meeting, on the sidelines of a soccer field—anywhere. Remember, women you meet will play a unique role in your life. They all may not have the capacity to listen empathically to your stories; however, each, in her own way, will contribute gifts to your life. Stay open to who they are and resist the temptation to be critical or judgmental. Through their connection, each will help you to heal and reveal a special, maybe hidden, part of yourself.

Divorce motivates women to transform their lives because it removes them from their reliance on one person, one man. When you were married, you may have developed a kind of complacency where you allowed most of your world to revolve around the needs and desires of your husband and your families. Divorce provides the opportunity to cultivate relationships with women who meet very specific needs, but who may not be compatible with other parts of your life. Transforming your life so that you live in accordance with the multiple whims of your personality requires that you encourage yourself to search for and connect with all different kinds of women. This is a fun journey.

The Ways of Women's Friendships

The ability to form friendships doesn't come naturally to everyone. Developing intimacy is something that you may not have learned in your younger years. Fostering deep friendships—the kind of relationship that feels like sisters—takes time and patience to create. It takes skill and an understanding of the nature of women, friendships, and connection. The following section will help you to create this kind of deep, woman-to-woman support system. Many women learn how to do this for the first time during their postdivorce years when they hunger for close (level 2 and 3) relationships with women.

If your satisfaction rating on the friendship index of the Pillars Exercise was less than a 10, you might want to consider utilizing some of the skills and knowledge outlined below to increase the joy and support that your friendships currently are affording you.

You Will Not Be Liked by Everyone

Anytime you reach beyond the world that you know, you are taking a risk. Transformation requires that you summon your courage and do this, and yet divorce makes you vulnerable to hurt. What should you do? Amy wondered how to become friends with women at the local PTA. She noticed that small groups of women would go out for coffee after the meetings, but she was never invited. She had initiated phone contact with women in the group several times. They were always warm and polite. She even spoke with a few while waiting in the school carpool line, and yet none responded positively to her overtures to get together socially. It's important not to label experiences such as this as "rejection," but rather as some sort of "incompatibility." Something about Amy did not feel consistent with the kind of friends that the PTA women wanted to bring into their lives. Try not to personalize these situations. That is, don't start believing that there is something "wrong" with you.

Amy explored whether there was something that she could do differently when she was with the PTA ladies. She hoped that she could discover something new about herself that would help her connect with them. This questioning process is a brave and important activity on the road to transformation. The lesson for Amy was this: to accept herself, her strengths and weaknesses, and the different ways she might come across, and to know that there will be people who, for one reason or another, choose not to affiliate closely with her.

You will not be attractive to everyone, nor will everyone be attractive to you. When this happens, move on to meeting new people—and there will be other people. Dwelling on what didn't happen is a mistake and can cause you to become stuck. Keep walking forward and look for new people, experiences, and activities. (A side note: This same lesson will be important to you should you decide to begin dating.)

Initiate Contact—Don't Wait to Be Called

It feels so nice to be called and invited to an event doesn't it? Unfortunately, this doesn't seem to happen as frequently as most people desire. Instead of feeling rejected and frustrated when the phone doesn't ring, call others. Realize that when you initiate, you have power. Recall the discussion in chapter 2 on being powerful. Calling others allows you to choose the person and set the place and time for your connections. Women often seem passive about initiating social contact, even with other women. Therefore, if you call other women, especially single ones, they probably will be thrilled to hear from you. On any given Friday evening, there are hundreds of delightful, single women alone in their homes wishing that they were engaged in a fun activity. All of them have reasons why they are not willing to initiate contact. Call. Connect. Make exciting, fun plans. Your life will be richer because of your initiative. Transformation requires that you take charge of your life. Opening up the channels of connection in yourself and with other women will allow you to create the kind of social network and friendships that will bring joy, support, resources, and companionship into your life. Don't sit back. Reach for what is important to you.

Enter Connections Gently

Unless you reflect on the way you are approaching friendships, you might be so focused on you own fears of rejection that you give little thought to the experiences of those with whom you want to connect. Most individuals greet new people with some feelings of vulnerability: Will I be liked? Will this person judge me? Will I be hurt? These thoughts makes the first contact with new women a very fragile time. Each party scopes out the other, hoping to reveal some cues whether the unfamiliar person is someone with whom it is safe to connect. These initial moments are important. Women look for signs of equality, similarity, and collaboration. They turn away from behaviors that connote that you are somehow "better" than they, or that you want to control them in a way that will compromise their own inclinations. Most women look for a willingness to be sensitive to their needs. This can be communicated by

- ♦ A gentle, warm invitation to connect
- ♦ Ability to say "No thank you"
- ♦ Gradual relating
- ♦ Curiosity about their lives
- ♦ A welcoming spirit
- ♦ Validating comments

♦ A soft voice

♦ A smiling face

♦ Asking permission to join conversations

When you are at an event in which you see a woman who possess the characteristics of someone you might want to get to know, approach with a new awareness, understanding that your behavior during these beginning moments communicates your sincerity and safety as a potential friend.

Friendships Require Attention

Friendships are like beautiful flowers, they must be watered continually or they will die. That being said, you may have some very special relationships that began in college or your childhood. You may not speak with your friend for years, and yet you are able to pick up the relationship exactly where you left it. Daily relationships with newer friends are different: they will continually sustain you, transform you, and help you thrive as you emerge from the upheaval of divorce. As such, they require more consistent care and attention. Although this may be difficult during busy times, it is particularly important that you regularly stay in touch with your women friends. Connections are deepened when you make a phone call just to say hello or to check in. Continuity and attention strengthen your bonds.

Balance How Much You Share and How Much You Inquire

Some women are so excited about getting together with new acquaintances that they jump on the opportunity to engage with someone else and spend the entire time speaking about themselves. Needless to say, you wouldn't be too anxious to connect with these types of self-absorbed women more than once. But self-disclosure is a very important part of creating connection. In fact, speaking about yourself, as opposed to current events or even about your children, will help you develop intimacy. If the focus of conversation is too much on you, however, you will convey disinterest in the other person and push them away. Attention to this balance is important. Ask questions; draw the other person into conversation. The more dynamic the give and take, the deeper the bonding will become.

People Differ about How Much Intimacy They Want

As you create new friendships, you want to listen for cues that tell you about the other person's comfort level. For example, if you begin to talk about a personal topic and your companion becomes silent or changes the subject, she may be telling you that she isn't ready for this level of self-disclosure. If you want to keep this woman as a friend, it is important that you honor her signals and retreat to a discussion that is more impersonal. On the other hand, many relationships with women progress toward deeper levels of sharing and intimacy. This is facilitated through the communication of caring, compassion, emotion, and curiosity. Many women depend on one another to help them explore their feelings and situations, and they value a friend's questions that display a sincere desire to help.

Women's conversations seem most valued when sharing occurs at an emotional level (both at the joyful and sad points of the spectrum), where both women feel genuinely heard and understood by the other. Joan Baker Miller, in *The Healing Connection* (1997), calls this "mutual empathy." She says: ". . . mutual empathy . . . creates the flow and change, the progression. Because each person can receive and then respond to the feelings and thoughts of the other, each is able to enlarge both her own feelings and thoughts *and* feelings and thoughts of the other person. Simultaneously, each person enlarges the relationship" (29). Thus the give-and-take of ideas, emotions, and experiences creates a special container in which each woman can grow and transform.

Be Wary of Overgiving

Women have a tendency to be givers in relationships; their gifts range from a well-timed telephone call, to an e-mail card, to a tangible "spontaneous" present. For many women, gift giving seems to come naturally. Giving can add a wonderful air of caring between friends, especially during divorce when one or both women may be experiencing a lack of nurturing from many other people. Too much giving, however, can overwhelm a relationship and cause the recipient to feel inadequate in her inability to match the gestures. Too much giving may lead a person to wonder about your motive.

Gloria did some deep soul-searching regarding the issue of giving to friends. Initially she thought that her impulses to volunteer favors or deliver surprises came from a very generous nature and desire to help people. She began to realize, however, that she sometimes also gave to receive something herself. For example, under the surface, she hoped that her gift would "buy" friendship, compliments ("You are the nicest person I have ever met"), or security ("I would never leave someone who gives me so much"). Thus, her gift often was met by disconnection instead of the intimacy for which she was hoping.

Generosity must emanate from a sincere and unencumbered space for it to be received in the intended spirit. Before extending a gift of any kind, check in with yourself and ask, "Why am I wanting to give this token?" If your motivation is to bring joy, surprise, or warmth to a friend, and there is no other motivation lurking below the surface, then you can enjoy the connection that comes with caring about someone enough to want to bring a smile to his or her face.

Be Sensitive to the Inclusion and Exclusion of Others

As you start to know more women, you will do things together and share resources, ideas, support, and activities. Being among a consistent collection of friends and acquaintances creates a sense of belonging and is extraordinarily healing. Whenever possible and appropriate, extend invitations to others to join in. Many women have felt so wounded by petty exclusion in their adolescence, that a spontaneous phone call to come along can begin significant healing. Many women who begin their postdivorce journeys as relatively solitary individuals are transformed by positive experiences with other women who invite them to be a part of a larger group of friends.

In the process of moving ahead and creating new parts of yourself, you occasionally will stumble across old wounds that require attention. Pain from times in your developing years when you felt separate and different from those around you may resurface when you meet new people and face the possibilities of forming new connections. If you attend to this vulnerability within yourself and other women by mindfully staying aware of the impact of inclusion, healing and transformation will occur.

Don't Let Competition Destroy a Friendship

Friendships and groups are rarely free from the influences of competitive feelings. This subject is often overlooked regarding women's relationships, and yet it is almost always present. Unfortunately, women rarely are taught constructive ways to express and manage competitive feelings. As a result, these normal emotions often become channeled into actions that hurt others or diminish a woman's self-esteem.

The desire to hide competitive feelings seems to stem from the belief that connection is best fostered through sameness. The more characteristics, beliefs, and preferences that you share with another woman, the more likely you are to bond. This association becomes challenged when circumstances (either perceived or due to a particular situation) demand that one woman be chosen or preferred over another, such as in competition for a job, male attention, or selection to a club. When this occurs, the security of a relationship or a group seems threatened. Reacting defensively by somehow diminishing the status of the other woman then leads to disconnection with everyone involved.

What would it look like if you transformed your experience of competition and made it an occasion for deeper connection instead of a time of negativity and disruption? Years ago, Heather joined a large women's organization. There she met a woman who possessed many of the same strengths that she saw in herself. At first, Heather felt drawn to create a friendship with this woman, and then, later on, as their relationship developed and they both occupied similar positions in the women's organization, she noticed herself wanting to diminish the other woman in the eyes of the others. She began to gossip, remark on the other woman's smallest flaws, and confer with a small group of women who would affirm Heather and discount the other. Needless to say, the friendship declined and the community began to experience the effects of the conflict. As the stress of the competition increased, it was evident that neither woman (nor the group at large) was benefiting from the competitive dynamic; there was no reason why either woman had to be perceived as better than the other.

They realized that they had to talk about their feelings of competition or risk not being able to competently facilitate group events. They discovered that there was plenty of room at upcoming events, as well as in the community at large, for both of them. Each of them, in her own way, had unique contributions to offer. By finding ways to complement each other's actions, instead of trying to diminish each other, they found themselves ultimately happier and more successful. This insight led to a mutual admiration of each other and a recognition of the similarities and differences between them.

By finding ways to blend and appreciate your different personality styles, create space for everyone's gifts, and accept that there are going to be times when one person is preferred over the other (and that this does not diminish your value), you establish friendships and take pride in one another's accomplishments. Transforming competition from a win-lose event into a situation in which you acquire new information ultimately enriches your relationship with yourself and with others.

Be Aware of Your Capacity to Hurt Others

As you engage in the dance of connection, you inevitably will step on some toes and prefer some "dance partners" more than others. Maintaining compassion and concern for those with whom you are not compatible allows you to proceed through this vulnerable time with a deeper appreciation of women. Each woman you interact with, whether or not you choose to move toward deeper levels of intimacy with her, possesses an important lesson for you to learn. It may be found in her strengths or her shadows. By being gentle and kind to all women, you cause no harm and, at the same time, become more open to learning and growing.

Revenge, jealousy, and maliciousness shut down the vital energy of transformation. Sometimes, you may not be aware of these feelings until you inflict pain on another. If you examine your impulses to minimize women whose personalities or behaviors feel uncomfortable to you, and understand these desires as reflecting undesirable parts of yourself, then your transformation will expand into new, revealing directions. Acting with compassion contributes to your journey as a divorced woman in two important ways: it allows you to facilitate the growth and healing of other vulnerable women, and, at the same time, provides you with new venues for self-reflection.

Lessons, such as those just mentioned, are the fuel that feed your transformation. Although learning and attention to growth can become wearisome at times, the outgrowth of finding new ways to experience life with joy and fulfillment is intoxicating. If reaching out to women is a relatively new experience for you, give yourself permission to live on your "growing edge." Try to put your fears to the side and initiate conversations. It is through taking risks that you will uncover gold. Relationships with women are among the most valuable treasures that can come to you during this transition period of your life. Women will bring laughter and hugs as well as help you reclaim some of the most beautiful parts of yourself. Reach out to one woman at a time. Approach her with an open mind and heart. Your efforts in this area will yield the most bountiful rewards.

Creating a Place for Transformation

When you undergo a traumatic event, it's natural to seek safety wherever you can find it. For many women, that means finding sanctuary in the solitude of your own home—a place that is familiar, a place in which you can close the door, lock it, and prevent the potential intrusion of more rejection, pain, and disconnection. While time on your own may serve a protective and contemplative function, it also may prevent the wounds of shame and fear from being healed through new experiences and new relationships. During the vulnerable and transitional passage of divorce, close relationships with women are very important. These connections will nourish you, guide you, teach you, hold you, push you, and give you new outlets for fun and play. Why walk the path alone when you can have companionship? You want to move beyond past disappointments and create new sources for affirmation: positive networks, friendships, and communities provide the support that you need to greet the next phase of life with wisdom, strength, and excitement.

Chapter 4

Creating Clarity

People change in two basic ways. One way is called *incremental change* (Quinn 1996), which is exemplified by women who view their divorce as an event that happened *to* them. They see their circumstances as outside of their control. While they pursue new relationships and new activities, there is a strong likelihood that these women will return to many of the same dissatisfying behavioral patterns (such as the way that they related to others) that plagued their predivorce lives. The emphasis on just altering circumstances is typically not enough to produce life-enhancing change and long-term happiness.

A second model of transition is *deep change*. Quinn said, "Deep change differs from incremental change in that it requires new ways of thinking and behaving. It is change that is major in scope, discontinuous with the past, and generally irreversible" (1996, 3). This type of change takes a lot longer to accomplish and often does not result in "feeling better" as quickly as you might like. It involves the courage to look within yourself and develop new knowledge of who you really are. Armed with new self-awareness, you can journey into the future with new tools, understandings, and strategies with which to build a future that is substantially different from the past and has the potential for lasting happiness. Women who are willing to spend a period of time devoted to introspection, either on their own, with other women, or with a therapist, will emerge from the passage of divorce with an increased sense of confidence and self-esteem. They will have accumulated a fund of new knowledge and skills with which to build a more satisfying future.

As you approach the threshold of your transformation, it is important that you reflect on the kind of change, deep or incremental, that you want to make in your life. The model that you choose will determine the kind of actions that you will take as well as the time frame in which you can expect to experience your transformation. Although deep change takes longer and is usually more challenging, it will assure you a life that is different from your past and one that is most likely to provide you with the joy you most desire. In this chapter, you will learn the first step toward creating deep change.

Debriefing the Past

Deep change requires that you break your connection with past patterns of thought and behavior and open to new ways of conducting your life. To do this you must gain an understanding of the intricacies of your personality and how your actions and emotional undercurrents impacted your marriage. *Debriefing* your past by asking questions about your motivations, intentions, and beliefs when you were married will help you understand who you were when you were married, and enable you to create clarity about ways in which you would like to transform.

It is tempting to keep the focus of investigation on your spouse. This protects you from the pain of seeing your own imperfections. However culpable he might have been in the demise of your marriage, analyzing his behavior will not further your mission. The clearer you become about your own inclinations in relationships, particularly intimate ones, the more you'll be able to discern more satisfying courses of action in the future. The greater your knowledge about yourself, the less likely it is that relationship difficulties will happen "to" you. Instead, you will have developed the tools necessary to significantly impact your directions and choices.

The Debriefing Process

In the pages that follow are powerful questions and lessons that inspired transformation for many divorced women. First, thoroughly answer in your journal each of the listed questions. Do this before reading further. Then, each question will be followed by a bit of wisdom that has been gathered throughout years of other women's experience. (The growing never ends!) Read this section many times. Each reading can open a new door of awareness for you. Make notes in your journal as you consider the questions. Chronicle the thoughts that you ponder, the questions that arise, and the insights that allow you to think of yourself in new ways. You might want to reserve several pages in your journal for each question so that you can return to a particular issue and expand and deepen your exploration.

Consider the various questions from as many vantage points as you can. Discuss your ideas with people who know you well or ones who have taken similar journeys. The more reflections you collect, the vaster will be the wisdom that will serve you in the future.

As you progress through the questions and discussion, you may notice yourself becoming emotional. This is a very important signal that the issue at hand holds particular importance for you and may deserve further and deeper exploration. Consider the following reactions as "red flags":

◆ You feel sad, angry, frightened, or guilty.

◆ You feel defensive.

◆ You keep the focus of your recollection on him and not your own behavior, feelings, or experience.

◆ Your self-reflections are interrupted by the thought that you are "right" as opposed to asking "What other ways could I have handled this?"

◆ You continually see yourself as a victim.

◆ The phrase "I am a failure" keeps coming up.

◆ You focus on the details of what happened, the story, as opposed to how you felt and what choices you might have had.

◆ The task of debriefing feels easy.

♦ You keep going over the same points and issues, as if walking around in a circle.

If you are signaled with a "red flag," try to examine what thought or memory may be triggering the feeling. These are the areas that probably hold some important lessons for you. Reassure yourself if you become worried. If you reflect on a situation where you realize that you caused a rift in the relationship or you chose a direction that ultimately brought a great deal of pain into your life, embrace these realizations. It is appropriate to regret the impact of some of your behavior as long as you also celebrate the notion that now, armed with a new piece of self-knowledge, you will be less inclined to travel this same road in the future. (That's great news!)

Ten Questions of Clarity

The process of creating clarity is different for everyone. Questions that are powerful for one woman may be less powerful for another. Issues that may spark the curiosity of one woman may be dead ends for another. Differences notwithstanding, the following questions are a helpful starting point for your debriefing:

1. What was your understanding about the nature of connections as you grew up?

2. What did you think you wanted from a relationship?

3. What attracted you to your husband?

4. What warning signs did you miss when you chose your mate?

5. How well did you foster connection and partnership?

6. How did you handle the differences between you and your mate?

7. How did you cope with the hard times?

8. How would your husband describe you?

9. How do you assess your behavior as a mate?

10. What feelings and thoughts has the ending of your marriage brought up for you?

Five Clarifying Categories

The questions are divided into five categories to help you organize and then integrate your thoughts:

1. who you were before the relationship began

2. the factors that enabled you to choose the relationship

3. how you handled maintaining connection in the relationship

4. who you were as an individual in the relationship

5. your experience at the end of the relationship

Remember that the key to finding and learning your lessons is to stay focused on you. Try not be distracted by the actions of others.

Before the Relationship

Understanding the woman you were when you met the man who was to be your spouse will enable you to gain a perspective about your receptivity to the kind of marriage you created.

Most people begin relationships completely unaware of any of the factors that will influence their relationship choices. They meet a man and "fall in love." Think, for a moment, about the word "fall." When you "fall," do you have control over where you fall, how you fall, the impact of the fall, and so forth? Do you ever even want to "fall?" How would your relationships be different if you chose to "step" into a relationship—if you made a clear, thought-out choice about with whom to create a relationship? Sure you might still make a mistake and wander into a hidden hole, but injury is less likely to come from "stepping," than "falling."

What was your understanding about the nature of connections as you grew up? It is almost a cliché to state that your childhood experiences influence your life as an adult, and yet the people who you lived with in your formative years, and the way people around you connected and interacted with you and with each other, formed a template for your adult relationships.

Spend time in your journal intricately describing each of the key relationships in your childhood. How did you see your parents connecting? How did they express their love for each other? How did they express their disagreements? (Red flag: If you answer that your parents never fought, look more closely. All couples have times when they disagree. If you do not remember seeing this as you grew up, it is important to find out why and what was really going on.) Focus on the nature of connection among all of the pairs on your list. What did you learn about the nature of connection and disconnection? Is it constant? Does it come and go? Is it intense? Is it punitive? Is it loving? Is it too close? Is there room to be an individual? Is it accepting?

In summary, at the point just before you met your spouse, what did you believe (from experience and modeling) about the nature of connection and how it develops in a relationship? What you knew in this domain (most of which was unconscious at the time) set the stage for your marriage.

What did you think you wanted from a relationship? Go back to the time in your life just before you met your husband. What do you recall thinking that a relationship would be like? What were you hoping a relationship would bring into your life? Here are some responses that other women have shared: "I have always just wanted to be a wife and have children"; "I needed to move out of my parents', house and this was the way women did that"; "I wanted to share my life with someone"; "I wanted to be with someone who truly loved me"; "I wanted to be a part of a family"; "I met Tim and we were in love; Marriage just seemed natural."

As you reflect on your motivation to become married, see if you can discover any areas of vulnerability that you might have hoped would be taken care of if you were married. For example, were you afraid to be alone, did you feel unlovable, did you not want to feel pressured to earn an income, did you want the status that being with a man, or a man from a certain background, would give you? These kinds of issues are called *blind spots*. Most people have them to some degree and they're often hidden behind romantic notions of being in love. Unfortunately, they usually resurface and cause problems.

Typically, the seeds of these vulnerabilities were planted in your childhood. Because you had not found a way to take care of these insecurities yourself, you unknowingly searched for someone who you believed would take care of them for you—a spouse. Problems arose rather quickly because no matter how wonderful your partner may have been, he couldn't resolve the issues for you that you hadn't resolved yourself. If you weren't aware of this dynamic, you became angry at your spouse because he wasn't fulfilling your unspoken expectations—expectations about which you were not even aware—thus irresolvable marital fights occurred and distance began.

For example, a very successful executive woman had been continually angry with her husband while they were married. Their most frequent fight concerned her resentment of his involvement with various soccer teams, a hobby that he had before they were married. Immediately on their separation, she began to have intense panic attacks that she said arose because she hated being alone. On reflection, she realized that before she met her husband she was consumed by school or working or dating. She was rarely alone. "I didn't get married to be alone on Saturdays," she said. Now divorced, she was forced to deal with being on her own and learning how to depend on herself for companionship—a lesson she came to embrace after a lot of painful work.

Needing a relationship because of insecurities and fears—as opposed to wanting a relationship without demands—starts a marriage with a major weakness. Understanding the factors that may draw you to needing to be married will help you keep this vulnerability in check so that you can begin future relationships strongly.

Entering the Relationship

The beginning of relationships is exciting and emotional. You can be so distracted by intensity and passion that you discount or fail to notice warning signs that indicate this relationship won't produce the growth and happiness you desire. Debriefing your experiences allows you to clarify what factors pull you toward relationships that you later find to be neither viable, healthy, nor capable of sustaining the challenges of time.

What attracted you to your husband? One divorced woman had a successful dating revelation. She said with unbridled enthusiasm, "The key to identifying the 'right' man is this: If you are at a party where there are ten men, eliminate the three that you are most attracted to, then eliminate the three that you are least attracted to. Get to know the remaining four." This woman has wisdom! What she learned, through many disappointing relationships, is that the emotions that propel her to be attracted to or repelled by a given person are misleading. She is right. These feelings are generated by a psychological phenomenon called "projection." Imagine an old-fashioned movie projector, the kind where there are reels of plastic pictures and a light that throws the images of the pictures onto the screen. Your psyche works the same way: it takes images of your positive and negative past experiences (especially ones about which you are unaware) and projects or attaches them onto new people you meet. You respond to particular people (in either a negative or positive way) because they are familiar, because they carry projections of experiences from your past. Therefore you may be drawn to a man who is like your father, or a man who behaves in a way that you were told as a child is "bad," but you never really understood what was so "bad" about those actions. Projection is a very complicated concept. What is important to understand is that projection causes unexplained attraction as well as repulsion.

To learn from your past so that you can move into the future with strength and hopes of making better decisions, you need to create clarity on what draws you to certain people—what are you projecting? You want your choices to become ones that are consciously thought through and not based on unexplained passion. You know a woman is caught in the web of her projections when she says, "I don't know exactly what I like about the man, but I do know that I feel wonderful when I am with him."

Moving ahead with strength requires that you do know why you like the people with whom you choose to connect—that you relate first with your minds and then with your feelings. If this sounds "unromantic," you are right. Choosing a healthy marital partner involves considerable thought, not passion. Sol Gordon, author of *Why Love Is Not Enough* (1990), discusses the idea that you'll find many people whom you can "love," but you will find fewer people with whom you can create a strong, viable partnership.

Now is a great time to become clearer about what attracted you to your husband. As you review the first minutes, hours, days, and weeks of knowing your former spouse, become clear about what drew you to him. Allow yourself to consider any of the features that he might have shared with either of your parents. He might have been like them, or he might have had characteristics that, as a child, you wished your parents had. When choices are based on childhood experiences as opposed to conscious adult wisdom, they typically are unsound.

A Transformative Exercise. In your journal make a list of the positive and negative attributes of each of your parents. You may want to add lists for any other adults with whom you were close as a child. After you have made very thorough lists, circle the three most positive characteristics and three most negative characteristics of each parent.

Remember, a characteristic may be an attribute that a parent did *not* have. An example of this might be a father who did not have time to give you the attention you wanted. Next make a list of all of the characteristics that attracted you to your husband. Are there similarities in the lists? There are for most women.

The existence of similarities between your mate and your parents is not a bad thing unto itself. The key is learning to think through your choices and become aware of what characteristics are indicative of a healthy mate, instead of allowing yourself to be magically attracted to someone. That *magical attraction* is an example of "falling" in love. The future goal is to choose with more deliberation and to "step" into love.

What warning signs did you miss when you chose your mate? The phenomenon of projection is also responsible for blinding you to characteristics in a man that might mean difficulties down the line. For example, Judy, a very bright, seemingly aware woman, was involved with a very abusive man for eight years. None of her friends could understand why she chose to be with such a man. When they continuously confronted her about her choice she responded that they did not know him as she did and that he was truly a wonderful, loving man. She discounted the actions of his belittling her in public and yelling at her often by saying that these actions were really "no big deal." She was blind to the red flags of abuse.

Judy's clarity came when she realized that, while she had a very loving father, she always felt that there was something not quite right with her. Her dad didn't pay as much attention to her as he did her other siblings. Choosing a man as a mate who frequently reprimanded her for making mistakes and for whom she had to continually work hard to earn his love, attention, and compassion set up the circumstances that she had felt as a child, although to an extreme—that she just wasn't good enough to merit a man's attention. This realization brought her choice-making criteria to her awareness—attraction was being driven by her childhood needs to try harder. What she knew as an adult, however, was that all people, including her, deserve to be loved and treated kindly.

When Judy reflected on her thought processes over the eight years of her relationship, she marveled at how she rejected the feedback of her most trusted friends and she wondered if she could ever rely on herself to make well-conceived choices when it came to men in the future. She decided that while she was learning to think through her choices more rigorously she would ask her friends for their input about the men she dated and use their feedback to illuminate characteristics that she had a tendency to leave in the dark.

To help you gain more clarity about your projections and the impact that they might have on your choices, ask your friends and your family their opinions. Listen carefully to what they might say and watch any tendencies you might have to be defensive. Use their thoughts to stimulate your own thought processes about how you select people to connect with and whom you are attracted to, and see what lessons you want to consider using in the future.

Sustaining Connection

While relationships of all sorts probably consume more time and attention than any other single activity throughout life, we don't generally receive systematic instruction about how to develop and maintain healthy connections. Therefore most women enter marriage doing the best they can to be a productive, positive partner, and yet miss the mark simply due to inexperience or lack of knowledge about how to keep relationships vital and alive. Creating the kind of clarity that will promote more satisfying relationships in the future requires that you review your behavior within the marriage and ask what you did that helped the marriage and what you might have done to weaken it. This type of inquiry takes courage as it will mean that you identify and accept responsibility for problems that you may have unwittingly created. Of course relationships require input from both parties. The behavior of both individuals must be considered as contributing to a relationship's development and downfall. Although examining your own behavior and identifying your "mistakes" takes courage, the more you can discover areas for your own improvement, the greater will be your potential transformation.

There are many components in a relationship that warrrant valuable self-examination. The three that follow deserve significant consideration.

How well did you foster connection and partnership? Another way to ask this question is: What did you do to nurture your partner and the relationship? In any relationship there are three parties that require attention and consideration: me, he, and we. With busy schedules and huge demands it's easy to forget that the mainstay of a healthy relationship is to take care of it.

Relationships require more care than most people realize. In addition, most relationships take the gifts of each partner for granted.

How often did you thank your partner for his economic efforts? How often did you compliment him? How often did you thank him for doing chores, putting the children to bed, or taking care of the lawn or car? Many women respond to these questions with, "Why should I thank him for activities that are his responsibility?" The reason is that the more appreciation there is in a marriage and the more recognition there is of the efforts that each person contributes toward the family, the stronger a relationship becomes.

Every Friday afternoon, for example, Stephanie's husband brought her a few roses, the kind that may be bought from a person at the side of the road. After a while, she felt that the roses were a habit and not a gesture of affection. In addition, despite all of her invitations, her husband spent very little time with her. As a result, she began to interpret the flowers as a way to placate her and not as a gift. "I know I should be appreciative of the roses, but I feel so ignored in the rest of our relationship I just cannot say 'thank you.'" This marriage eventually died of neglect.

As you create clarity around the extent to which you nurtured your partner and the relationship, even during the difficult times, notice how much you were willing to give and how absorbed you tended to be with your own needs and concerns. Finding ways to open pathways for more generosity may be an important area for learning and growth.

How did you handle the differences between you and your mate? The differences between marital partners often form the battlefield of the relationship. Think of the most significant difference between you and your former spouse. What angered you the most about the difference? How did you react when you were confronted with them? What happened to your connection with your spouse when these differences surfaced? Typically, differences pull spouses apart. Each fights for his or her way of doing things or his or her preference as if each would lose themselves if their notions were not utilized or attended to. With this kind of attitude it is no wonder that marriages are fragile.

Learning about your strengths and weaknesses in a relationship will be enhanced when you consider the pivotal role that you allow differences to take in your relationships. People tend to react to the presence of differences in one of two ways—they are either *accommodators* who give in to the will and preferences of others or they are *fighters* who insist that their will be done or threaten to withdraw and disconnect if their desires are not embraced. Accommodating and fighting are opposite ends of the same road, and they force members of a couple to see preferences and interests as a forced choice—his way or her way.

You can learn a great deal about yourself by noticing your tendency to see the world in terms of opposites and by observing any inclinations that you may have to resist other ways of thinking about an idea or pursuing an activity. A major piece of transformation could occur for you by shifting your viewpoint from a world of "one way or the other" to a world where many different ways have merits. In this latter paradigm, options are seen as exciting opportunities to experience something new, vehicles through which each member of the couple has a great opportunity to learn and grow.

A Transformative Exercise: In your journal, explore the following questions: What role did you allow differences to play in your marriage? What about the existence of differences caused you to resist, pull back, or judge? What kind of changes would you have to make within yourself to welcome differences in a relationship instead of fighting them? As you journal your answers to these questions, allow yourself to feel a shift beginning within you—from a woman who felt restricted in the presence of some differences between herself and her mate, to a woman who has crafted a way to allow these same differences to propel her toward personal expansion. This shifting represents an important transformation and will serve you tremendously in the future as you become a woman who warmly, authentically, and vibrantly creates connections with a diversity of people in various situations.

How did you cope with the hard times? How difficult times were handled in your relationships has a lot to teach you. How did you express disagreement with your spouse? How would you characterize the way you argue? When your spouse was not as attentive as you would have liked, what did you do and how did you feel? Were there recurrent themes in the topics and issues during the painful and contentious times?

The hard times hold golden lessons. The fact that you feel vulnerable during altercations signals that you're dealing with issues that are raw from childhood or with topics or feelings that are so unfamiliar that you feel uncertain about how to respond. Many people look back and characterize their behavior during these times as "childlike." They yelled and screamed, called their spouse mean names, ran away, became silent, withheld love, closed down emotionally, became passive-aggressive, or stayed angry and distant until they got their way. Does any of this describe you?

As you think back to these times, see if you can trace those feelings back to similar experiences from your childhood. You may remember times when your parents fought or when your mother ignored your father. You may remember times when you were reprimanded by your parents and not allowed to express your feelings. Claire, for instance, promised herself that she would never allow herself to be stifled as she was when she was a child. Not surprisingly, she never backed down from an argument in her marriage, even when she knew, inside of herself, that she was wrong. This awareness is very important, as you might find that the moments that were difficult in your marriage were more about issues that you could not resolve with your parents than issues with your spouse. You may have unconsciously chosen a marital partner who would give you a long-awaited opportunity to resolve an issue with one of your parents.

Katherine, for example, married a very busy executive with whom she had little in common. She found herself annoyed with him constantly about the amount of time he spent at the office. When she described her marriage, she said that she should not have been surprised that he was a "workaholic" as he worked long hours before they were married. This woman recalled that her father had similar behaviors, but that, while her mother was unhappy with this pattern, Katherine was forbidden from confronting her father. "I guess that when I yelled at my husband about his work hours, I finally had the chance to speak my mind," she said.

As a divorced woman, you have the opportunity for deep personal work and transformation by debriefing your marital confrontations and opening yourself up to excavating the lessons hidden in the rubble of the endings of your marriage. By removing the resistances and exploring the multiple issues that were present during each contentious event, you can begin to understand why you fought or ran as you did. With these new realizations, you can reconcile many of the painful concerns that have been acted out in more current relationships and lessen the probability that they will interfere with connections in your future.

A New View of Yourself

A critical feature of the debriefing process is to focus intensely on who you were in the marriage: How did the marriage impact your feelings about yourself? What did you learn about your vulnerabilities and your strengths? What have you come to understand as the best of your personality as well as the least attractive parts? If you have the courage to really use your marriage as a powerful mirror, you will be able to see important reflections of who you are and what you have to offer a future partner. This is vital data that provides you choices for how you may want to transform yourself as you consider what kinds of relationships, with both men and women, will enrich you during the next phase of your life.

How would your husband describe you? The ideal way to receive input as to how you were as a mate is to ask your former husband how he experienced you as a wife. However, it isn't always comfortable or possible to ask your former spouse personal questions. If you could, though, the following would be helpful: What did you like the most about having me as your wife? When was I the most difficult to relate with? What do you see as my greatest difficulties? How do you think that I contributed to our marital difficulties? What could I have done differently to bring us closer together? If you could have changed me in any way what would it have been?

It is difficult to even think about these questions without feeling defensive, and yet the more informed you are about how others experience you, the more options for growth and change you will possess. Of course, you don't have to agree with any feedback that you are brave enough to solicit. In fact, you must rigorously consider whether a particular piece of feedback is important to you. Your scrutiny is your power; it is the way you take control over your own transformation and make sure that you grow in the directions that are aligned with your philosophies, beliefs, and values.

A Transformative Exercise: If you are not able to interview your former husband, which is likely to be the case, there are three options, all of which require creativity and dedication to the truth:

1. You can write a dialogue in your journal where you allow yourself to answer your questions as you truly believe your former husband would have answered them. The more you can be honest, the more helpful the exercise.

2. You can ask someone who knows (or knew) your husband well to answer your questions as he or she honestly believes your husband would have answered them. This will require

that you vigorously assure the person that you will receive his or her input calmly and that you will not condemn him or her for the responses.

3. You can interview many people that you know, asking them how they believe your husband might have responded. Explain to these individuals that you are seeking as much constructive information as possible. They will not serve you by withholding sensitive feedback or by telling you that you did nothing that would warrant change.

However you choose to engage in collecting information, make sure that you are gentle with yourself—do not be overly zealous in your pursuit to the point of feeling bad about yourself. You will know that the exercise is creating helpful information when you feel a bit uncomfortable, anxious, or even defensive. This will mean that you are hearing new information and exploring unfamiliar terrain. Remember, none of the input means that you are "bad." You may learn that you are incompatible with individuals with certain characteristics or preferences, which is great information to use when you seek out new connections.

You will, if you did the exercise thoroughly, learn about parts of yourself that have yet to fully develop, areas that may not have matured beyond their childhood or adolescent modes of expression. These are great areas for potential growth. There may be moments when you feel bad, sad, shame, or regret. When this occurs, reassure yourself that you are a growing, developing woman and that no one is immune from behaving "imperfectly." Most of all, if you begin to feel down, take a moment to acknowledge your courage for being open to scrutiny and remind yourself that each relationship provides an opportunity for learning and growth. Your marriage was such an experience. All of your future relationships will also challenge you to grow. Pain accompanies transformation. Now in possession of this new information, you are on a strong path toward new possibilities.

A Transformative Exercise: Here are some questions that may start you on a journey to evaluate yourself as a spouse. It is likely that your responses to the questions will expand over time, so it is wise that you keep space in your journal to continue your exploration of each area. Add more questions, move into new directions, and be as thorough in your quest to understand your experience of your marriage as you can.

♦ What are some valuable lessons I learned from the marriage?

- When did I feel the most vulnerable in my marriage?

- When did I feel the most empowered?

- What gifts did I bring to the relationship?

- When did I contribute to the difficulties?

- What were the most difficult times for me in the marriage?

- What circumstances brought up my anger?

- When was I not as honest as I could have been?

- To what extent was I able to share love openly?

- To what extent was I able to disagree openly?

- Within myself, what blocked me from expressing myself?

- What activities did I not pursue because of the marriage?

- What special dreams did I not pursue because I was married?

- In what areas did the marriage help me grow?

- What do I wish I had done differently during the marriage?

- What made me a "good" partner?

- In what ways was I and was I not a nurturing partner?

- To what extent was I an open, sharing partner?

- In what ways was I a selfish partner?

These questions can inspire you to explore the whole experience of yourself within the relationship: your feelings, behaviors, boundaries, dreams, philosophies, strengths, and weaknesses. The more deeply you can engage in this self-study, the greater will be your capacity to transform.

Endings

The American culture has a phobia about endings. Department stores move from one holiday to the next before consumers have time to put decorations away. As students finish one level of schooling they are rushed on to the next with little time for closure with teachers, lessons, and classmates. Popular entertainers and politicians come and go. We are not given the chance to say "goodbye" and thus are left wondering, "What ever happened to her or him?" Society is sadly lacking in rituals that mark the end of time and provide important moments for reflection. Therefore, the last important question in this chapter:

What feelings and thoughts has the ending of your marriage brought up for you? Most women answer with one word: fear. The fear that many experience on divorce is related to their discomfort with disconnection. Connection is the single most driving force in women's development (Miller 1997). Most women do not strive as rigorously toward independence, a topic that will be explored in a later chapter. Therefore, when a primary relationship is over, the female psyche becomes shocked. One woman who was miserable in her marriage said, "I couldn't stand living with him; however, knowing that he was in my life was a kind of comfort that I miss."

When your system feels jolted, fears arise: concern about being able to take care of yourself, concern about never experiencing love or sex again, and issues about not knowing how to spend time on your own. Preoccupation with outer appearance may arise when a relationship ends as well as concerns about growing old. These are very important issues that may have stayed dormant when you were in a relationship, as if the marriage protected you from having to think about them.

Allowing these issues to clearly surface during divorce will shed clarity on areas to which you have not attended. Addressing these areas will help you gain strength as a growing woman. As you focus on what you are feeling, take notice of your thoughts about being a single, independent woman. Make a list of all of the areas that you question your competency to handle. Instead of shrinking back from the items, step forward. You have just become clear about the challenges that lie head. This list comprises new areas to explore, great directions for future growth, and exciting transformations.

As this chapter closes, think about the story of *The Wizard of Oz*. You end your marriage feeling as if your house has been hit by a tornado and you landed in Oz. Maybe the witch under the house is your former partner; maybe the witch represents the darker parts of your personality that have plagued you for years and have needed to die. The questions and answers that will arise in the debriefing process are your Yellow Brick Road. If you allow yourself to follow it, you will meet friends and allies along the way who can guide and teach you.

New witches will cross your path and demand that you choose between their fate and your own. Ultimately, your journey "home," that place of love and belonging, has always been within your grasp, but it requires that you walk the entire path to learn that lesson. Follow your Yellow Brick Road. Ask the questions to create the clarity you need to understand where you are and where you want to go. It is through this exhausting yet rewarding trek that the location of your next destination will become clear.

Chapter 5

Embracing Independence

Right after I was divorced I had the occasion to go to a doctor's office where I had to complete a form asking for my vital information: name, address, phone number, and so forth. I stopped at the box that read: "single, married, divorced, separated, widow." I didn't know what to choose. I was very surprised by my emotional reaction—I became angry. "I'm not going to check any of these boxes!" I heard myself say. What was going on with me? "I am none of these things!" the voice within continued to rant. This was one of those moments when personal reflection is important. I realized that I resented being asked to label myself with respect to my relationship with a man: "It is none of their business!" I tried to engage this rebel within in a dialogue. "How would you like to respond?" the calm, rational part of me inquired. There was silence. The maverick seemed stumped. And then, with a quiet knowing strength, the answer floated into my awareness: "Independent."

Take out your journal and write down the phrase, "I am an independent woman." Say the phrase over and over. Record all of the thoughts, feelings, and images that come to your mind as you say this phrase. This is how a group of women responded to this statement: "I see a woman out there, on her own, and lonely." "I see a woman doing what she wants to do, when she wants to do it, going through life on her own." "Makes her own decisions." "Has her own money." "Is very strong." "Doesn't have children." "A career woman, very successful." "Hard. Unemotional." "Doesn't have men in her life." "Has her own opinions and is not afraid to express them." "Does what she wants, but people don't like her a lot."

It is interesting to note the visceral responses. On the one hand, there was a glow in their eyes as if independence was a valuable, sought-after prize. And yet, this reaction was immediately accompanied by a darker reaction. While independence could yield freedom of thoughts and actions, it often also meant not being connected with others, not having an attractive personality, not living an emotionally satisfying life that included love, family, and close friendships.

What does this mean about the programming many women possess? Perhaps women have allowed relating and independence to exist at opposite ends of a continuum and, in so doing, made it psychologically difficult to pursue the kind of life that encompasses all of what they want: love, relationships, freedom, opinions, career pursuits, lifestyle preferences, and so on. As divorced women, the apparent incompatibility between independence and connection is a quandary— do you develop the inner capacity to be independent and live life on your own, or do you "hold out," and wait for a new relationship to come along?

It is clearly time to develop a new paradigm. Among the gifts of divorce is that it provides an ideal opportunity to discover your own, unique ways to blend independence and connection. Living on your own, now more mature than before you were married, you must learn ways to take care of yourself, provide for yourself, and create a life that is prosperous and happy. Simultaneously, as you feel ready and if you deem it desirable, you can begin to initiate connections with men and women and mold them to conform to a value system that appreciates the needs of the individual as well as the needs of the relationship.

Connecting with women was addressed in chapter 3; relating to men will be discussed in chapter 10. This chapter explores you and the ways you can expand your capacity to be in relationship with yourself—independent. This must begin by confronting a perspective that women often learn in the earliest stages of life: that it is essential to take care of everyone before you consider your own needs. When a woman accepts herself and her needs as important and is willing to conceptualize, create, and maintain a life that is productive, meaningful, and enjoyable to her, then she experiences freedom and joy in all sectors of her life. This chapter will focus on ways to claim and develop this fundamental commitment to your desires and sense of purpose.

Separating and Finding What Is Yours

Everyone marks her day of separation differently. To some, it is the day you decided to end your marriage, even though the physical separation might not have happened until weeks or months later. For others, your separation occurred on the day that your husband told you that he was leaving, or maybe the day that he told you that he was thinking about ending the relationship. While there may be different indicators of "the end," women seem to have a common experience concerning the impact of the separation. This can be described as the *Velcro effect,* a phenomenon where two items that were once intricately interwoven pull apart only with some difficulty. So, too, do many women struggle with shifting their consciousness from that of being part of a pair to that of being a single person. Women tend to create their identity around those with whom they feel close, especially their spouses. For example, women have a tendency to describe most of who they are and what they possess as "ours": "our home," "our vacation," "our family," "our decision," and so on. There are very few areas in their lives that most women think of as exclusively their own. Careers are often the major—and sometimes only—focus that women claim exclusively as their own. Even the decision to diet, move to a new place of employment, or purchase a new dress, many do in consultation with their mates and proclaim, "We decided."

Among the first transformational tasks, therefore, is shifting the perspective from "we" and "ours" to "I" and "mine." This represents a major change. Of course, Jumpers leap onto this new role with great exuberance—some moving into "my own apartment"; others wearing the clothes that "I want to wear" for the first time ("He always hated blue!") Ponderers move more slowly, wanting to make sure that they are comfortable with the new choices that they are making. Whatever your style, divorce affords you the exciting and frightening opportunity to own and take charge, maybe for the first time, of your life—your home, your body, your spirit, your money, your time—and transform them to reflect the essence of who you are and who you want to be. Your divorce can also give you the chance to find a way to arrange the building blocks of your life so that they support you, in your own unique way, as you embark on your quest to be a growing, vibrant woman who is seeking to make her dreams become her reality.

How Independent Are You?

The following brief questionnaire will help you assess the degree to which you act, think, feel, and make choices independently. Tune in to your thoughts and feelings as you answer each item. If you become aware of wanting to qualify your responses or if you notice yourself having a reaction to a particular item, record these thoughts in your journal. The more you understand the issues that surround your comfort level with being an independent woman, the clearer you will become about how you want to transform this piece of yourself.

Independence Questionnaire: A Transformative Exercise

1. When you are planning a weekend, how much of your time is dictated by the needs or desires of others and how much is determined by what you want to do?

2. When you are faced with making a decision, how much input do you seek from others?

3. How comfortable are you doing activities on your own?

4. How often do you try something new, something you have never done before?

5. How do you feel when faced with a day where everyone you know is busy?

6. How easy is it for you to disagree with the opinions of others?

7. If a famous person whom you really admire was making a presentation in your town and no one wanted to go with you, would you go alone?

8. How often do you find yourself in conflict with others because they are not doing what you want to do?

9. How often are your decisions based on the opinions of others and how often are they based on your own preferences?

10. When you are facing a difficult situation do you reason it out on your own or do you seek the counsel of others?

11. When you need something, do you ask others to provide it for you or do you find ways to provide it for yourself?

12. How often do you feel hindered in living your life the way you would like to because of the actions and choices of others?

13. Do you know how to perform basic maintenance on your car?

14. Do you know how to balance your checkbook?

15. Do you know how to mow the lawn?

16. Do you know how to cope with the breaking of household appliances?

17. Do you know how to videotape a television program?

18. Do you know how to file your taxes?

19. Do you know how to pay the tip in a restaurant?

20. Do you know how to make a major purchase such as buying a house or car?

Look at the answers to these questions and any reactions that you may have had to any of the items.

- ♦ **Items 4, 7, and 11** help you assess to what extent you are willing to act on your own and how much your activities are dependent on the company of others.

- ♦ **Items 6, 8, and 10** provide you insight as to how dependent you are on the thoughts and opinions of others; your ability to form your own opinions of situations; and how well you think through the best solution to challenges.

- ♦ **Items 3, 5, and 12** assess your comfort level with being on your own. These questions ascertain how you feel when you are alone, and when you rely on the actions of others.

◆ **Items 1, 2, and 9** uncover your ability to make choices based on your own needs and desires and how much you make decisions based on your preferences as opposed to trying to satisfy the desires and opinions of others.

◆ **Items 13 through 20** give you the opportunity to begin to take stock of your capacity to attend to the nuts and bolts of your life—knowing how to do things and where to get help so that those mundane chores can be completed without relying on the expertise of others in your life.

Tools of an Independent Woman

Acting independently, making choices based on your own desires and beliefs, thinking independently, feeling comfortable when alone, and having the skills and knowledge you need to take care of yourself—these are the essential tools of an independent woman. These tools can be applied to living on your own as well as when you are in a relationship. The context of your living situation is not as important as is your orientation to yourself, your needs, and your desires. Independence is an inner commitment to be aware of your needs, opinions, and desires, and to continually pursue ways to consider and accommodate these needs.

Independent Action

Doing something on your own is difficult for many women, be it travel, going to a gathering of new people, or even exploring a new part of town. This is especially true for women who became adults during or before the 1970s, when independent action was not a part of the way you were raised. Where most boys are encouraged to explore, compete, build, and meet challenges with a tough, "John Wayne" sense of adventure, girls are usually more sheltered. They are inspired to seek out relationships, get along with others, fit into the group, and be sensitive to the feelings of others. Girls are often not prepared to conceptualize or develop a life on their own or a life that reflects individual desires. Researchers report that girls are taught to avoid taking risks and instead seek the security of people and situations that are familiar (Austin 2000). For divorced women, this is important to realize. It means that you have been programmed not to act independently and that you have little or no experience with taking independent action. No wonder so many women become frightened, sometimes to the point of panic, when faced with time alone.

If you are ready to seek transformation in this area, there are several steps you can take:

1. Develop a list of activities that you can do on your own. Begin the list with an activity that would be relatively easy for you to take on your own (call this a level-1 activity) and end the list with a pastime that seems so huge, impossible, and risky that you can't imagine ever doing it solo (call this a level-10 activity). For example, the first item might be going to the ice cream store and enjoying an icecream cone by yourself. The final item might be going to an isolated beach house by yourself for one month.

2. As you feel ready, attempt to accomplish an activity at a moderately difficult level on your list. Repeat pursuits at this level of risk until you feel comfortable with the action. Then move up one level to a slightly scarier activity.

3. Engage the support of a friend or coach to help you plan your approach to each level and to celebrate your accomplishments with you.

4. Always have an "out." If you begin an activity and find yourself not able to tolerate the anxiety involved with this new action, be sure that you can retreat to a place of safety. Never shame yourself for backing down. Give yourself points for trying. Continue to approach the new situation. Your anxiety will diminish as the action becomes more familiar to you.

Mastering the skill of independent action takes time to evolve. Be patient with yourself. Take small steps. Pushing yourself to experience gradually increasing levels of risk will teach you to tolerate the anxiety that comes anytime you do something new. Over time, you'll learn that you can trust yourself in a new situation and that you are safe when you take independent action. This reflects tremendous growth. Remember your goal: to be able to pursue all of the activities and directions that you desire regardless of whether you do them alone or with others.

One woman who tried the above exercise said, "If I feel comfortable going places on my own, why will I need a partner or a spouse? I will be too strong and no man will want me." These sentiments are common. "Needing" a companion places constraints on a relationship.

It lays the groundwork for disagreements, resentments, and anger, such as when one member of a couple wants to spend a Saturday playing golf and the other wants to go to a craft show. If each needs the other to pursue his or her activity, a conflict is inevitable. Conversely, when each member of a couple knows that his or her participation is not needed, but rather that it enhances the experience of the other, then the freedom that is experienced by each individual brings the partners closer together. When each knows that they have the choice (as opposed to pressure) to join in, greater closeness is created.

Divorce is such a fertile time for growth. When you were in a relationship you may not have had the "push" that you might have needed to figure out what *you* wanted and then act on your own. Encouraging yourself to go to a movie on your own, go to a party on your own, take a vacation on your own, or move to a new town on your own will help you expand your interests, your circle of acquaintances, and the opportunities available to you. Great transformation is possible when you open up the doors and walk through. Take one step at a time. Your world is waiting.

Independent Choices

Making independent choices and decisions presents a particularly difficult challenge. Not only is it a risk, which may be uncomfortable, but making sound choices also requires having knowledge that you may not possess. As with independent actions, learning to trust your decision-making skills will grow with experience.

Forty-year-old Amanda had been separated for two years when her divorce settlement was finalized and she found herself in a position to buy a home, for the first time, on her own. Not knowing where to start, how much she could afford, what mortgages were, and the like, she approached her father for help. His initial response was to laugh. "You're not considering buying a house," he said. "You can't afford it, and suppose you want to remarry soon, then what will you do? It's not wise for a single woman to own her own home." This response confused Amanda as she had anticipated his support. Amanda was a hard-working professional and single mother of two children. She knew of other women in similar circumstances who had purchased lovely homes, and yet her father's advice brought up a lot of doubts within her. She had always thought of her father as someone who was wise, whom she could rely on to "take care of her." Now what should she think?

With the help of a coach, Amanda gathered information and other people's points of view before making her decision about whether to rent or buy. She spoke with friends first and learned about how they proceeded in similar circumstances. This led her to speak with an accountant and a real estate professional. Both helped her review her financial situation and provided her with data to consider. Now, armed with information, she was better prepared to make her own, independent decision. Amanda bought a moderately priced townhouse. During the closing on the home and for the first several months she was living in the house, Amanda felt very anxious about her decision. She found ways to respond to her inner self-doubts and gradually become comfortable with her decision and happy that she was a homeowner. This story ends with a somewhat humorous note: one evening at a large family gathering, Amanda overheard her father proudly telling a relative that, "My daughter is one of those 'women of today.' She owns her own home and needs absolutely no help from anyone, although she still calls me for advice from time to time."

Making independent choices does not have to happen in a vacuum. You never have to be alone with your decisions. Wise decision making, no matter how experienced you are, typically involves gathering data and speaking with others who have experienced similar circumstances. Utilizing the services of relevant professional consultants (doctors, lawyers, accountants, and so on) will help you gain the confidence that you have thoroughly explored and considered every possible scenario.

While making independent choices does carry a lot of responsibility, it also gives you power over the direction of your life. Thinking through options and then making informed decisions are the vehicles that will carry you toward your dreams. Will your choices and decisions always be the right ones? Probably not, and you must be prepared to make mistakes and not judge yourself harshly. Before making a major choice, imagine yourself in the future looking back at the moment that you made the decision. Then ask yourself two questions:

1. Have I done everything that I can to make the wisest decision at this time? (If you answer no, then do whatever is needed to answer in the affirmative.)

2. Can you think of anything that you have done that you may regret later? (If the answer is yes, do what is required to reconcile the regret.)

The answers to these questions will give you the assurance that you have done the best that you can at the time. You cannot expect more from yourself.

Making independent choices is a growth experience and, as with all other areas of being independent, may cause you to feel anxious or fearful. Often women feel that these emotions are telling them that something is wrong. Typically, however, uneasy feelings indicate that you are doing something new and unfamiliar. If you have done your homework, as described above, you can rest with the assurance that the discomfort is the normal feeling most people experience when they are taking a risk. These risks are necessary for your growth. They will move you along the path toward transforming your life. When you develop a wise decision-making process versus making spontaneous decisions in a vacuum, then you will be able to trust yourself more and more. With experience, making independent, life-fulfilling choices will be easier, empowering, and even fun.

Independent Thinking

The ability to think independently is tied to your capacity to tolerate differences between yourself and others and your past experiences of expressing your opinion. Take a moment and reflect back to your childhood. When you expressed your point of view, what was the reaction of the adults around you, particularly your parents and teachers? Were your opinions respected? Were they welcomed? Were they encouraged? See if you can remember specific times when you shared what you were thinking. Perhaps you had a reaction to something you were watching on television. Were you ever at a family gathering where you overheard a relative express an opinion that you challenged? Typically children speak their minds until they are taught that it is not safe or acceptable to do so.

Maria, a thirty-seven-year-old woman who is an executive assistant in a large firm, decided to become a vegetarian when she was around nine years old. She had heard someone speak on the television about killing animals, and from that point on she did not want to eat meat again. When she told her parents they laughed at her, told her that she was being ridiculous, and said that they would not cook specially for her. She dreaded having dinner with the family because they would try to force her to eat meat, and when she refused they told her that she was not respecting her parents. This caused Maria to become very shy.

Interestingly, Maria married a man who was very outspoken. Their marriage began to deteriorate when she disagreed with him about how to raise their children. He yelled at them frequently. Maria's love for her children and desire to protect them "forced" her out of silence.

Maria's discovery is very important and may be one that sounds familiar to you. It does not occur to children to evaluate their parents' points of view; they assume that their parents are right and they, as children, are wrong. The way parents model how to handle differences creates the framework for the future. Some families relish debate and encourage opinions to be expressed. Other families value individualism and encourage their children to "be their own person." Other families are very hierarchical and dualistic. They present the world as black or white, right and wrong. These families, typically, do not tolerate the expression of various points of view. Do you see a pattern in your family?

Adolescence is another important time when girls may learn to steer away from independent thinking. During this period of life, the desire to fit in with peers and be a part of the group is a girl's primary concern. Researchers have found that unless teenage girls are educated in a setting where they feel safe, comfortable, and encouraged to speak out, they become silent, minimize their intellectual pursuits, and seek connection at all costs (Gilligan 1993). During adolescence, you may have learned that connection and independent thinking (and action) are incompatible. With this belief, you create your first male/female relationships, which may reinforce the pattern. As one fifteen-year-old girl said: "If you disagree with your boyfriend too much, he will say that you are bossy and break up with you."

Being divorced and on your own is a great time to revisit the value you place on independent thinking and speaking your mind. Identify women who express their opinions and who have a personality style that makes you feel comfortable. Some women see Oprah Winfrey and Rosie O'Donnell as powerful models of women who are warm and also forthright. Make a list of what the women whom you admire do that differentiates them from women whose personalities you judge as "too strong." Examples include: "They always seem gentle, yet clear." "When someone says something they don't like, they disagree with the idea not the person." "They never yell when they disagree." "They use phrases like 'that doesn't make sense to me,' 'I hear you, but I don't agree,' or 'I wouldn't do it that way.'"

Experimenting with different ways to think independently and express yourself is an important part of this transformational period. As with other areas of creating independence, finding a style in which you feel comfortable will take time. Here too, you initially may feel anxious and uncomfortable. Expressing your own viewpoints may feel as if you are taking a huge social risk.

You must discover on your own to what degree you feel comfortable sharing thoughts that are different from those of the people around you as well as how you want to communicate your ideas. There will be times when such expressions will cause distance or a rift between you and others. During these difficult times, taking the initiative to honor your companion's conflicting opinions—agreeing to disagree—demonstrates that the connection between two people transcends the varying ways that they may think. This action also shows that lively, respectful debate provides an opportunity to learn something new. Of course, there are individuals who have to always be "right." Differing with these people can result in an uncomfortable power struggle. You may choose not to be very close with these people, and maintain them as acquaintances, not friends; or you may choose to curtail discussion when controversy occurs.

While independent expression is a choice that you make depending on the situation and a particular relationship, independent thinking is an important way that you honor yourself as a woman. When you give yourself permission to reflect on what is important to you and what you believe, you deepen your bond with yourself and expand your awareness of the choices of action that are available to you. Choices lead to freedom and an expanded sense of power. Transforming toward a greater capacity to think independently allows you to create a life that accommodates your deepest desires and moves you to enjoy higher levels of satisfaction and personal meaning in all that you do.

Independent Feeling

Some of the difficult feelings that accompany independence have been briefly explored throughout this chapter, namely anxiety, anger, and fear. For many, divorce brings up profound feelings of insecurity—the sting of failure, the pain of disappointment, the fear of the future, the panic of the unknown. Few women escape a period of wrestling with these feelings.

Enid, a very successful businesswoman, felt a great deal of shame surrounding the panic she felt about living alone. "If anyone at work knew what a baby I am at home, they would never believe it," she often commented. In fact, Enid had had very little experience living independently. "I went to college after high school and always lived with a roommate. Then I went on to graduate school where I lived in a group house with other students. I met my husband at the end of graduate school and we moved in together right after graduation. I guess I have never lived alone," she admitted. "On the evenings when Bob was away on business, I would keep myself so busy at work that I would drop into bed when I got home. I now realize that I must have used work to avoid being alone. I sure got a lot done during those evenings!"

Anxiety, or emotional vigilance, is the defensive system's natural reaction to being on guard when approaching a new experience or an unpredictable situation. If you have not spent a great deal of time living alone, it is normal to feel trepidation. The key to learning to cope lies in how you interpret this physiological reaction. Most women are taught to seek safety, protection, or reassurance when they feel nervous. This message, usually taught by parents, communicated that you were not capable of taking care of yourself. Ironically, those from very loving families often received the message to be careful and be safe to an extreme, when supportive, protective parents swooped into any uncomfortable situations and rescued their children from fears. If this is familiar, imagine how you might be different today if instead of being coddled and protected, you were reassured that you could handle a new situation, and then were lovingly pushed by your parents to cope on your own. Boys are more typically raised in this fashion than are girls. In addition, boys are encouraged to not lean on their parents, to seek adventure, and to leave the safety of home. Girls, on the other hand, are often not pushed out of the nest (although this is becoming much more common). They often are expected to stay sheltered within the family system until a man appears to take care of them. Therefore, many women face divorce unaccustomed to life on their own. Feelings of insecurity are inevitable.

If you can understand the roots of your discomfort, you can begin to reassure yourself. As a child, you would not have been capable of surviving on your own. Now when you're scared, it's common to revert to childlike thought patterns. Self-assurance begins when you remind yourself that you are not a child, but a capable adult who possesses many skills and competencies that will enable you to survive on your own. What are they? Complete these sentences in your journal: "I can physically take care of myself by . . ." "I can emotionally take care of myself by .. . ."

Some answers will include earning money to support yourself, discovering activities to entertain you, or identifying resources to educate and support you. Remind yourself often that you can live independently; that you will not only survive, but thrive. The words that you say to yourself and the self-caring actions that you take will gradually teach the little girl who still lives inside of you that she is loved and that she is safe.

Fear into Excitement: A Transformative Exercise

Try this sequence of thinking to transform your fear into excitement:

1. "My anxiety arises when I am confronting a new situation."

2. "New experiences are the pathway to growth."

3. "Therefore when I feel anxiety I must be growing. Growth and transformation cannot occur without some level of anxiety."

Now when you become aware of the fear in the pit of your belly, you still may feel uncomfortable, but see if you can also find feelings of excitement that remind you that you are headed toward the future that you have been working so hard to create. This thought sequence will allow you to maintain momentum toward your dreams.

Independent Skills and Knowledge

Two weeks after her husband moved out, Suzie was on an emotional merry-go-round, yet determined to successfully live on her own. She went downstairs to check the laundry and was shocked to discover a huge flood of water all over the floor. She didn't want to panic; she wanted to handle the situation. "Discover the problem," her voice of reason inside instructed. She went to the drain and removed the lint and dust that had accumulated. Motivated by her independence, she cheerfully grabbed the mop, wiped up the floor, and began a second load of wash.

When Suzie later went to check the laundry, she couldn't believe the flood had returned! Becoming frustrated felt like a sign that she wasn't truly independent, so she again tried to discover the problem. She twisted the water lines and cleared out the hoses with fresh water. She took out the clean clothes and did a test run of the water cycle. Nothing backed up. All was well. She had fixed it this time! Tired but pleased with her emotional accomplishment as well as with fixing the broken washer, she again mopped up the floor and placed her last load of laundry into the washer.

Thirty minutes later Suzie went downstairs to retrieve her laundry and the washer had overflowed again. Rationality left her. She screamed an obscenity, began to cry, and called her now former husband to come over and fix the washer. He came within the hour, put his hand into the machine, pulled out a sock that was interfering with the interior drain, and left the house, all within a five-minute period of time. Suzie's anger and frustration was more than she could describe. She resented having to call him. She resented her lack of knowledge that kept her dependent.

Suzie was determined to find ways to become self-reliant. She learned that independence grows through two types of knowledge:

1. Knowing how to do things.

2. Knowing who to call to get things done.

It is important that you remember that you have a choice about which option to choose. Learning new skills is key to this piece of your transformation. Consider taking classes or reading books about money management, simple home repair, gardening, and computer work. Dedicate time to practicing and advancing your new talents. It can be fun! Expanding your capacities to take care of yourself will breed enormous self-confidence. As your abilities progress you can even use them to barter for chores, such as trading baking, carpooling, or babysitting for help moving furniture, splitting wood, or doing a job that is unfamiliar to you. Trading fosters and advances your feelings of independence. While you might not know how to do everything (who does?), you do have skills that you can use as currency with someone who has talent where you have limitations and vice versa.

Finally, learn how to use the Yellow Pages, classified ads, and recommendations of friends to find and pay for professional help. You might automatically think of people you know, such as your father, brother, or former husband, as the only people capable of helping. In other words, "running back home" seems to be the only option. This can make you feel incapable, weak, and very dependent, particularly on men. Paying for services is understandably not a preference, but sometimes it is a necessity. Knowing that you work hard and can pay or barter for help allows you to maintain your sense of yourself as a powerful woman.

Recognize, too, that you do not have time to learn and do everything yourself, although you may feel like Wonder Woman. And when you do pursue something on your own and you can see the tangible results of your labor, such as a painted wall or a weeded garden, these moments are important. They'll help you realize how much you have grown, and how capable and independent you have become since your divorce.

The Rocky Path of the Independent Woman

Many women say that becoming an independent woman has provided them with a sense of freedom and power in their lives that they did not experience before their divorce. This has changed the way that they connect with others, the way that they parent, their approach to their work, the expansiveness of their dreams and visions, and their capacity to be a life partner. It is as if they can now, finally, trust themselves to take care of themselves. Knowing about this inner capacity allows them to better cope with the bumps that life tosses in their paths. This doesn't mean that they like the bumps, but they know they can figure out a way to survive them and continue walking down the road.

No matter how extensive your transformation, there will still be times when you will feel overwhelmed and lonely. It is as if the little girl inside of you has had enough of being competent and independent, and cries out for someone to take care of her. When these moments occur

1. Contact your support system of family and friends who are available for encouragement and resources.

2. Give yourself permission to break down, and take a time-out from being mature and strong. Hide under the covers, or cry on the sofa. This response may be somewhat reminiscent of past weaker responses. Now, however, monitor your moments of self-doubt and exhaustion, and only allow the breakdown to continue for a limited amount of time. Then "get back to business."

3. Develop an inner voice of accountability that will speak out and gently call you back to the strong, independent woman you have become.

4. Encourage yourself to become active: create a plan, write in your journal, approach your tasks one step at a time, and so on.

These actions will allow you to become somewhat independent from the vulnerable parts of your personality. They'll help you remember your inner vitality that will sustain you and drive you forward.

In all, creating independence will reorient you to yourself and your life and give you permission to be *self-oriented,* that is, consider and act with respect to what is best for you. Self-oriented is not the same as *selfish,* which means you focus so much on your needs that you hurt others by your neglect. Your newly developed independence will thrust you into a mode where you continually are learning new ways to grow and take care of yourself. Your connections with others will improve tremendously because you will stop demanding that they take care of you and stop becoming angry when they don't attend to your needs. No longer feeling needy of others or entitled to being taken care of will make you a more attractive friend and mate. Finally, you will feel happier as you experience the inner power of knowing that you can create and maintain a life that is productive, meaningful, and enjoyable. This capacity, along with a firm commitment to yourself, will give you an expansive sense of confidence, strength, and freedom. Your visions are your future waiting to happen.

Chapter 6

Reclaiming Your Vision

Many divorced and divorcing women say they feel "stuck in the past." They say that they cannot stop thinking about their former husband (even if they have concluded that he is not the "right" mate for them), they feel depressed that the marriage is over (even if they believe that the marriage was unsatisfying), and they're unable to do anything but stay at home, go to work, and take care of the children (even when they admit that these limited activities are not productive or fun). It's as if there is a little woman deep inside who believes that dwelling on the past will somehow change it, or that feeling angry at a former husband will punish him for the pain he's caused. Sound familiar? These thoughts are irrational, and yet you may cling to them. They are a life-line to what is familiar, and they provide protection from entering new territory that feels risky and frightening. And yet, somewhere within, you know that if you don't venture along a new path you'll be doomed to a life defined by negativity, pessimism, loss, and deprivation.

Immobility is often caused by the belief that to change you must act right now. The immediacy of this expectation is scary, and so you run backwards to cling to the familiarity of the past. It feels more comfortable to hold on to an unhappy past than to step out toward an unknown future.

The key to reclaiming life and moving ahead lies in thoroughly, slowly, and sensitively preparing yourself for transformation. The first, foundational preparatory step is to create an exciting and alluring vision of the future. It's easier to begin a journey when you know where you want to go than by stepping blindly onto an unfamiliar road.

While the process of divorce is extremely painful and causes a great deal of upheaval, it ironically also provides an important gift: the opportunity to review your life and make "midcourse corrections" as to how you have lived. The process of creating a life vision helps you disengage from the past. It also challenges you to consider the various components of life and ask yourself the question, "If I could live my life in any way that I wanted, with whomever I wanted, where I wanted, doing what I wanted, what would my life look like?"

This chapter will lead you through a series of exercises and questions that will help you develop a thorough vision of your ideal life. While you may want to read this chapter and then move immediately ahead to the next ones, it is important that you understand that your vision will expand as you live with it. One idea or image will come to you and then, later on, you may be inspired to add more ideas. Allow the seeds of your vision to incubate and grow. The more detailed your vision becomes, the greater will be your motivation to move into the future. This is a fun, exciting, and energizing process.

Finally, as you work with your vision, expect to experience moments of anxiety and negativity. You may hear voices within you that say, "This process is silly. You cannot possibly achieve all (or any) of this." Or, "You are not smart enough (pretty enough, good enough) to achieve this kind of a vision." Or, "I can't do this; I don't know where to start." At this point, just put these voices to the side. For now, see if you can give yourself permission to allow all of your wishes and hopes to come to the surface. Invite them into your consciousness as old friends and welcomed playmates. Don't worry about whether they are reachable. Stretch to include any and all ideas that come to you—those that are old and have been with you for a while as well as those that you only now have conceptualized. This chapter will help you to weave them into a beautiful vision that will inspire and move you beyond divorce and into the future.

Wandering Mind: A Transformative Exercise

The conscious mind typically is occupied by present-oriented concerns. To get in touch with your deepest wishes, place aside your thoughts about children, chores, money, and the like, and let your mind wander. Retreat to whatever spot allows you to feel relaxed and comfortable to help free your imagination. A guided imagery is provided in the section that follows. The scenario is intended to help you imagine living your most ideal life. When you read or listen to the guided imagery, make sure you are relaxed and in a receptive frame of mind. There are several ways to do the exercise:

1. Read it to yourself several times. Record in your journal all thoughts and reflections that come to you.

2. Read the exercise into a tape recorder. When you feel relaxed and ready, get into a comfortable position, perhaps close your eyes, and play the recording back. When you are finished, record in your journal all images that you can recall.

3. Give the book to a friend and ask her or him to read it either into a tape recorder or aloud to you. When the reading is finished, record in your journal all that you remember visualizing about yourself and your ideal life.

Guided Imagery: Living the Life of Your Dreams

Find a very comfortable position and allow yourself to start feeling very relaxed. Take some deep breaths. Each time that you exhale, allow yourself to feel and release any tension that you may be holding in your body. Keep taking deep breaths until you feel relaxed and your mind feels free to wander and explore your deepest wishes.

Imagine that there is a slight stirring beneath you. It is a magic carpet that has come to take you on a journey into the future. Feel yourself sitting on it comfortably as you imagine it begins to move. The carpet gently takes you away from the place where you began this exercise. You become aware that you are entering a thick, warm fog. Although you do not know where you are, you feel safe and trusting of where you are going. You feel very soothed by the fog, and willing to leave your current life behind for the moment. The magic carpet ride continues, and you become aware that you are moving into the future. Even though you cannot see any surroundings outside the fog, you are confident that you are safe and moving toward someplace pleasant and wonderful. Your carpet moves ahead one year into the future . . . two years into the future . . . three years into the future . . . four years into the future.

Your ride slows and then stops. It is now five years from the time that you began the exercise. The fog lifts. You are sitting in a beautiful room, in a plush, comfortable chair. You look out a large window and see a star-filled sky. You feel relaxed, happy, and fortunate. You are home. It has been a wonderful day. You are filled with joy, love, and a profound sense of purpose in your life.

Notice the area outside of the window. What do you see? Where is your lovely home located? This is the home of your dreams, the place where you have always wanted to live. It is wonderful.

Turn your attention inside your home. Who else is living with you? Allow yourself to be aware of feeling fully happy and content, happier than you ever imagined was possible. Walk around your home. Notice your possessions, your decorations, and photographs. Enter each bedroom in your home. Remember the love that you feel for each person who has occupied these rooms. See their faces and remember the joy that you feel when in their presence.

Walk into the dining room, living room, and kitchen. Again, allow happy memories to come to you. How have you spent holidays? Who do you currently feel close to? Who is in your family, your community? With whom do you most enjoy spending time? Take a moment and think about the fun times that you are experiencing with the people in your life.

A book-type calendar on a table catches your attention. Go over and flip through the pages. What do you do during the day? You smile as you look at the activities that await you in the days ahead. You love what you do. Each hour of your day is very fulfilling. You feel productive, satisfied, and growing. As you turn the pages, you realize that your days and weeks contain a perfect blend of all of your interests, hobbies, and pursuits. You have enough money to spend your time exactly as you want. You have the kind of lifestyle that enables you to be completely happy and healthy.

As you return to your comfortable chair and gaze at the stars your realize that you feel a profound sense of peace and inner strength. How have you been able to develop such a wonderful life? What have you learned about yourself and your life over the past five years that has brought you to this blissful point in time? Think about the past incredible five years: the people to whom you have grown close, the experiences that have been the most gratifying, the accomplishments about which you are the most proud, the achievements that you were ultimately able to attain, all the parts of yourself and your life that you have been able to transform since your divorce. Close your eyes, take several deep breaths, and feel the joy that you have been able to create in your life during the past five years. Realize you've proven that you have the power within you to make your dreams come true. You are a strong and determined woman.

As you feel gratification and strength, the carpet beneath you begins to move. It is time for you to return to the present. Your magic carpet gently lifts you up, back into the warm fog and takes you back to the present point in time. The images and memories of all that you saw and experienced of your life in the future remain crystal clear as you allow your awareness of the present to return. You have returned to your current life. The feelings of having experienced your dream life remain within you, beaconing you to let go of what was and to begin reaching ahead.

Recalling the Possibilities

Taking the time to record the details of your guided imagery experience is important. Some of the images that you envisioned may not be new to you while other components of the vision may have come as a surprise. You may be tempted to discount some of the elements. For example, you may have sensed that you were in a relationship with a famous person or you may have been living in a huge, multimillion-dollar mansion on the beach. Regardless of how implausible your images may seem to you right now, write them down. Resistance to believing that dreams actually come true is common. Do not judge your dreams. Let them exist; they have been a sleeping power within you as you were dealing with your marriage and divorce. The goal in this chapter is to awaken the dormant parts of you and to help you identify dreams that call you to move ahead.

Feel free to embellish your visions as you write them down. If you envisioned one home and your dream is to have three, describe them all. If you imagined yourself as the vice president of a major company and you would rather be the president, write it down. If, as you are writing, you realize that your dream to be famous actor was missing from the visioning exercise, add it to your written vision.

The guided imagery was only a beginning and only one way to discover the elements of the life that you would like to be living five years from now. With the goal of seeing your life five years from now as completely as you can, you will next use other important sources within you to add to your vision.

Reclaiming Childhood Dreams

The period after divorce is a rich time-out from life as you knew it. Before divorce, you were probably focused on what was going to happen tomorrow, next week, and next year. Vacations and career paths were planned, decisions about whether to have children and where to retire were made, and maintaining day-to-day living required a great deal of effort. How often did you stop and ask yourself, "Is this what I really want to be doing?" or "Before the last day of my life, will I have tried everything that I wanted to try, visited every place that I have wanted to visit, and learned about everything that has sparked my curiosity?" The time after divorce—when the momentum of your life slows down considerably—is the perfect time to think about unfulfilled dreams and incorporate them into a new life vision. As you continue to create a vision about your future, go back through your life, particularly the years of your childhood and adolescence, and recall all of dreams that once brought a smile to your face.

Retrieving these important memories is an important journey in itself. You may best be able to remember your early years when you are engaged in conversation with other women about their childhood dreams. These discussions often trigger memories of moments in life that you have long forgotten. Other powerful ways to uncover memories are by looking at pictures, talking to family members, and reconnecting with childhood friends.

A Life Book of Remembering: A Transformative Exercise

The construction of a *life book* will help you recall many of your past aspirations and desires. You will need a stack of blank paper. Use one sheet for each segment of your life. Start by labeling one page for each grade that you spent in school. This may include preschool. For each year, note the names of your teachers, the school you attended, your age at the time, the names of your friends, activities that you enjoyed, and any achievements, struggles, or events that marked that time. Next, chronicle your life after high school by making a page for each further segment of your life. For example ages eighteen to twenty-one could be labeled "the college years" or "young adulthood." Other intervals could include times you lived in a particular house or location, worked at a particular job, lived in various cities, or spent time raising an infant. The purpose of these pages is to help you tune in to specific times in your life and recall the dreams and wishes that were important to you.

Once you have created this life book, answer the following questions on the appropriate pages as you would have answered them during each specific time in your life:

1. What do you want to be when you grow up? (What career direction is important to you?)

2. If you had power, control, and money, where would you like to be living?

3. If you had three wishes, what would they be?

4. If you could do anything with your life right now, what would you do?

5. What are three things that you would like to know that you do not currently know?

6. If you could wave a magic wand and transform your life, what would you turn it into?

7. If you could spend each day doing exactly what you wanted, what would you be doing?

8. If you could trade your life with anyone, living or dead, who would it be?

9. What individual, living or dead, do you most admire and why?

10. Describe your ideal spouse and your ideal best friend.

Filling out this questionnaire for each segment of your life is like digging for buried treasure. Somewhere, hidden within the answers to these questions, are unfulfilled dreams, values that guided your actions, activities that you wish you had pursued and maps to roads not journeyed. Write all unfulfilled dreams that you discover on a separate list titled "Dreams Deferred," a phrase from a favorite poem by Langston Hughes (1995). Record the age that you had this wish in case you want to refer to it later.

Reclaiming Lasting Dreams

Supplied with a long list of dreams that inspired and motivated you at different points in your life, it is now time for you to review the hopes that you have gathered and ascertain to what degree each one still holds your interest. Spend a few moments with each item on your list. Close your eyes and imagine this desire coming true in your life today. When you envision this dream coming into your life now, how do you feel? Do you feel excited? Do you feel "butterflies" or "twinkles" inside of you? As suggested during the guided imagery, fight the desire to judge or dismiss the dream. For now, your job is only to identify unfulfilled wishes. The challenge of how to actually bring them into your life must wait for the time being.

Putting Your Vision Together

It is time to return to the chapter 1 exercise, the Pillars of an Independent Woman's Life. In the Pillars Exercise, you evaluated your current level of satisfaction with the various aspects of your life and began to create an image of what an *ideal life* would look like. You now have more information about yourself and are ready to construct a more thorough, detailed vision of the various ways that you would like to transform your life.

Right now you are an independent woman. This does not mean that you are free from responsibilities, but it does mean that you are free to develop a long-term plan that is oriented toward your desires, and your dreams. (If, down the road, you choose to bring a mate into your life, it will be important that you choose someone who has a vision compatible with yours. If you're interested, there will be more about that in chapter 10.) Remember that you are crafting a vision toward what you will strive toward the rest of your life. There will be elements that you cannot immediately realize. For example, it may be that your vision is to live in a villa in Italy and paint pictures of the countryside. This type of move may not be desirable until your children are grown and living away from you. In chapter 8, Constructing a Transformative Plan, you will learn steps to take to move you toward living your dream.

Your task at this moment is to revisit each of the pillars. In your journal, write a thorough description of your ideal. Recalling the 1 to 10 scale, where 1 is completely unsatisfactory and 10 is your dream life, describe your perfect-10 vision. You began this exercise in chapter 1. Now, revisit what you wrote, expand your ideas, and gather all of your visions and dreams together. Use at least one page per pillar. Describe down to the smallest details each pillar as you saw it in the visioning exercise (answer the questions who, what, where, how, and when). Be sure to include plenty of color, texture, and movement in your descriptions.

Making Your Vision Even Grander

Your assignment thus far has been to create a perfect-10 vision. A 10 has been defined as the satisfaction level that reflects your most cherished dreams, regardless of whether you think that they are realistic or impossible to attain.

Many women's visions and dreams are not too grandiose in magnitude. For example, Ashley, who was a stay-at-home mother when she was married, said, "A 10 would be my having any kind of job that would allow me to pay the bills, put some money aside for the kids' education, and enable me to leave the house after my children left for school and return home before they got back." Ashley lacked confidence in herself. Any job was acceptable to her. She felt decadent dreaming about ideal work hours and wanting to have some money to put away. Many women are like Ashley: They have lost the ability to dream grand dreams; they don't have visions where they have more than they need or where they exceed expectations and reason. They hold back visions in which they are the heroine, boss, or lady of luxury. They block visions where they attain absolutely anything they want. Dare to dream about a life that is currently beyond your wildest expectations. Allow yourself to have grand vision in which you are living your bliss.

As your last visioning challenge, go back over each of your visions. You have described your level 10s. Now, kick back, roll up your sleeves, knock down the walls, and create *level-15* dreams. These are the dreams in which you can have anything that you want. "Anything?" some women ask with a tone that sounds like a little girl let loose in a huge toy store. Yes, anything. Allow yourself to play with your dreams. If you could have anything that you want in each category, what would it be? Release boundaries and limitations. Dare to dream!

It takes a lot of coaxing for many women to reach a real 15. Ashley, for example, finally described her level-15 dream like this: "I would love to design greeting cards. I did this all the time as a child. I would have my own greeting card company that was based in my house. I would employ lots of stay-at-home mothers. We would make cute, inexpensive cards for parents to give to their children any time they wanted to encourage them or give them a 'cardboard hug.' The cards would be carried in stores all over the world. I would make millions, have fun, not have to work very hard, have lots of help, own houses all over the world, and be able to spend lots of time with my children." She was ecstatic and energized.

Creating level-15 dreams may seem like a cumbersome task; however, you will feel enormous satisfaction when you are done. You will have a powerful sense of where you want your life to go. This vision enables you to construct a viable strategy and then take action in a way that most people are not able to do in their personal lives.

Interestingly, in the business and financial worlds very few people operate without this kind of plan. Action that occurs spontaneously, with no forethought, consultation, or planning is considered reckless. And yet, few people apply this same principle to their lives. If you follow the various steps outlined in this chapter you will gain a level-15 sense of direction and purpose. You will be able to answer important life questions—from what hobbies will bring you the most pleasure, to what kind of work you would excel at and enjoy, to what kind of a man you should date. It will help you feel motivated, excited, energized, committed, knowledgeable, independent, inspired, encouraged, enthusiastic, and resolved. There certainly will be times when you'll be afraid that you cannot reach your vision or when your vision itself will seem frightening and more than you can handle. (Ways to handle these insecure moments are addressed in the next section.) But most importantly, your vision of the future creates the framework for a plan that fills the empty spaces created by the divorce. Seeing yourself in new places, with new people, new activities, new competencies, and new possibilities, affirms the reality that life does go on after divorce. Joy, fulfillment, and satisfaction are not dependent on the existence of a given relationship, but rather on your creativity, desire, and will to pursue your visions and dreams.

Bringing Your Vision to Life

The power that your level-15 vision will have in helping you move ahead is dependent on your ability to bring it into your daily life. It cannot remain an exercise in a book or a journal; it must become an ongoing presence and influence in your life. The more you reflect on your vision and actively use it when making decisions, the more likely it will be that your life naturally progresses in the direction that you have delineated.

The more you bring your vision into your life, the more it becomes your reality. When your vision surrounds you, it is something that you think about, write about, and talk about—it becomes alive. Journaling is one way to help bring your vision to life. "Writing triggers the RAS [reticular activating system in the brain], which in turn sends a signal to the cerebral cortex. . . . Once you write down a goal, your brain will be working overtime to see you get it, and will alert you to the signs and signals that . . . were there all along" (Klauser 2000, 34).

There are many fun ways to become actively involved with your life vision. Journaling is only one. Here are other suggestions:

- ◆ Collect pictures of the place that you envision living some day and hang them around your house.

- ◆ Make a collage of images that represents various components of your vision. (This is a good exercise to do during the first week of January, too.)

- ◆ Talk to your friends and family about your vision.

- ◆ Create a folder for brochures, resources, and ideas related to your vision.

- ◆ Speak with people who are currently doing things similar to your vision.

- ♦ Research ways to become involved with aspects of your vision, such as schools to attend, real estate agents to contact, corporations who might hire you some day, matchmakers who might help you, or professionals to consult for guidance.

- ♦ Read books and articles about exciting aspects of your vision.

The point to remember is that the more you think about your vision, the stronger will be your connection with it. This will deepen your resolve to make it happen and motivate you to accomplish each step necessary to bring your dreams to life.

Creating a vision for the future may initially feel taxing and unwieldy. As you generate more ideas and develop more details, you will begin to experience an incredible sense of being alive, maybe for the first time in a while. Divorce and other traumatic times make life feel dark and heavy. These events stifle the energy within you that seeks joy, accomplishment, and love. Reconnecting with your dreams and believing in your ability to bring them into your life clears the air that was once heavy with grief, and enables you to rekindle the fire within your spirit. Now warmed by the thoughts of new passions, and illuminated with the hope of new possibilities, you are able to face the future energized, stronger, and ready to move ahead.

Chapter 7

Generating Energy

So far, this book has concentrated on your thoughts, your dreams, and your plans. At this juncture, it is important to focus on your feelings. What are you feeling right now? As you find yourself ready to walk into the future and move beyond the pain and upheaval of your divorce, it is normal to come to an abrupt emotional halt. Many women have described this sensation as falling into a huge pit, being blocked by a mammoth rock, or even being held captive by a tremendous giant. All capture the notion of being stuck in unhappy present circumstances with continuous thoughts and feelings about the painful past.

Howling at the Moon: A Transformative Exercise

Take out your journal and give yourself permission to *shout* your feelings and frustration. One woman called this exercise "howling at the moon." Push yourself to write continually for at least five minutes. Don't stop. Feel as if you are taking the top off a box that has been stuffed for too long. Here is a compilation of expressions from other women:

- ◆ This is all impossible! You may be able to do this but I can't.

- ◆ I am too depressed, too lonely, and too resentful.

- ◆ If it weren't for him I wouldn't be in this place.

- ◆ I hate where I am in my life. This wasn't what I wanted my life to be like!

- ◆ I hate him for what he has done and for getting on with his life.

Let all of your feelings out. Allow yourself to feel like a child and have what some might label a huge, out-of-control temper tantrum. Write all of these feelings down. This will help you reflect later on. You may find that you spew some valuable insights during these moments of rage and desperation. It's alright to let yourself go; it is cleansing, healing, and wonderfully self-serving.

This is a pivotal point for divorced women. You are facing one of the most important decisions in your divorce journey: whether to allow yourself to be held captive by the past or whether to cut the rope and free yourself to venture into your future. The metaphor of being tied up and held back is very descriptive of many women's experiences at this time. They meet suggestions of new activities with why they can't do them. The injustices and misdeeds of their former spouses dominate their discussion topics. Negativity and impossibility cloud their outlooks. They are lonely, sad, bitter, largely unproductive, angry, and feel victimized and unable to move beyond this spot. They have become immobilized and truly feel incapable of breaking free from this predicament. Do you feel similarly?

To Let Go or Not to Let Go

The drama around the question of letting go is profound. Many women stay stuck at this point and never embrace the glorious opportunities that await them at the next stages of their lives. Most women are rarely ever aware that they have a choice of staying inert or moving ahead. To move beyond divorce, it is essential that each woman, in her own way, resolve the stage of tension, confusion, and anger. This involves the mammoth process of letting go: letting go of some elements that define the past; letting go of anger and bitterness; and opening to the unlimited possibilities of the future.

This is not an easy task, to say the least. Just as it is during other times when you must let go (of children as they grow up, of youth as you grow older, of favorite jeans when the fabric has worn too thin to repair), you must grieve the ending of the time that was and walk courageously into the unknown. Without endings, transitions, and beginnings, it is inevitable that you will stay stuck.

The pages that follow explore some of the toughest issues that keep women frozen. Keep in mind that you always have choices about how to think and act. There is no right way and no right pace. Be true to yourself and the road will take you exactly where you need to go.

I Want My Life the Way It Was Supposed to Be

One of the most painful moments that all divorced women face is remembering their wedding day and recalling their dreams about the way "it was going to be." Based on the partner you chose, you had ideas about where you were going to live, how you were going to live, who was likely to be in your family, and so forth. Now, you face having to let go of the situations that surround those dreams (the people, the places, and so on), and you're most likely unsure if you will move toward a wonderful future without them.

Altering Your Standard of Living

The change in the standard of living experienced by many divorced women is harsh and dramatic. Often, due to their divorce settlement, many women no longer are able to have the same opportunities and material comforts that formerly brought them pleasure. It is natural to resist and to immensely dislike your new circumstances, and to voice sentiments such as

♦ But I don't want to work outside of the home.

♦ I want to stay living in this neighborhood.

♦ How will I afford the things that I have come to enjoy and rely on?

Many women voice these concerns as they feel entitled to maintain what was. The anger and sadness that accompany these changes are normal, honest, and important reactions. It is fine to feel these feelings and express them at times and places that are safe, private, and supportive. It is important, however, to realize that holding on to these feelings will keep you stuck.

When you are ready to move ahead (remember, each at her own pace) it will be necessary that you examine the feeling that often lies beneath: fear. Betty, a divorced woman, continually cried about having to sell her beautiful home; she masked her fear of the future either by talking about how special her previous home was or by telling bitter stories about her former spouse. She was furious about the new life he had begun to create for himself, and was enraged by the settlement that was bestowed on her by the court. She insisted that because her former spouse had wanted the divorce, she shouldn't have to pay by having a reduction in the quality of her lifestyle. They had no children.

One day, her dear friend Selma confronted her: "Stop talking about the past," she challenged. Betty slumped in her chair and sobbed: "If I couldn't talk about my old neighborhood, the vacations that I loved, and the promises that my ex made, I would have nothing. I have nothing!" She began to shake and cry a different kind of tears. "I will probably become a bag lady. No one will want me. I don't know where to go, what to do. As bad as it was with him, at least I knew who I was and where I was going. Now, I know nothing. . . ." She felt that all she had left were her debilitating feelings.

Fear is underneath a huge amount of sadness and anger. Letting go of past images leaves you with fear—fear of incompetence and, worse, powerlessness—to create the life that you want. Working with this fear is a key to moving ahead and will be further addressed in the pages that follow.

Being a Less Than Full-Time Parent

One of the most painful realizations for most divorcing parents is that they are going to have to spend time without their children. Regardless of the details of the custodial agreement, divorcing parents typically are confronted with the reality that their children will spend some significant time in another family system. This is perhaps the hardest part of letting go of the past. Women express in many differ-ent voices their agony and rage at facing this reality: "He didn't want to be a father when we were married. Now he is Super Dad." "He doesn't know anything about fathering. He lets them stay up late. He feeds them all kinds of junk food. They watch television all the time!"

The pain is expressed through judgment, critique, disagreement, and more. Many women cling to their opinions and observations as if these statements are the last lifelines that they have to time with their children. Although there is extreme heartache to this situation, it is compelling to examine how clinging to this anguish serves you. How does it make you a better mother? How does it help your children? In the beginning, your distress is the primal expression of the struggle to cope. As time, passes, however, the wound is no longer as raw (although the ache and longing linger).

How does clinging to your anguish serve you? It protects you from your fears—the fear that you will lose your children's love and that your identity as a mother is weakened when your children are with the other parent. These fears are intensified when a stepparent, girlfriend, or other person who potentially will receive love from your children is introduced. A sense of powerlessness drives emotions as well as the development of a void: who are you if you are not your children's full-time parent? The prospect of letting go of the images of how you would parent, how your family would function, and how you would experience the unique parent-child connection plunges you into the fear of the unknown. It challenges you with having to meet fear head-on to journey into your future. And yet, again, you have a funda-mental choice: to cling to a life that you will not have and feel the pain of being without it, or to risk letting go and opening to unknown possibilities.

Living on Your Own

Among the strongest and most natural drives that women possess is the desire to connect. Divorce jars women to their core when they must disconnect from the person with whom they have sustained a major life connection. For many women, the marital connection replaces the connections of a family of origin, including parents and sib-lings. Disconnection from the family of origin was easier because it went from one major day-to-day relationship to another and the marital rela-tionship accommodated even more areas of living than did those origi-nal family relationships. The ending of the marital connection is traumatic (even if you initiated the parting) because it begins life on your own—for the first time for many women—which can be a shock and can plunge you into yet another unknown existence.

A support group of divorced women discussing the topic of loneliness, anger, and grief commented as follows: "If I wanted to live alone, I would not have gotten married!" "I feel like I am on a deserted island with no hope of rescue." "When I come home from work I run to the answering machine. When there are no messages I feel tremendous despair."

The fear you experience concerning your changed standard of living, being a part-time parent, and living on your own causes a major stopping of the energy you need to grow, move ahead, and thrive. This profound challenge becomes elongated when you are unable, do not know how, or do not want to let go of the desire for your life to be just the same as it was before your marriage ended.

Acting Out Fears

Everyone acts out their fears in different ways. Some women immediately look for a replacement relationship and hope that it will enable them to move ahead again relatively unscathed; others go over and over in their minds the events of the past as if the retelling of the story will somehow change the ending; others hide by staying in their homes, burying themselves in work, books, television, or their children's lives; and still others do everything that they can to maintain fighting with their former spouse. This latter activity, when it involves attorneys and the courts, not only keeps women from moving forward (as their time and energy is occupied with lawyers, briefs, maneuvers, and depositions), but also severely and often drastically depletes their economic resources so that they are further hampered from moving into the future.

This is a sensitive, highly personal, and difficult dilemma for many women. When do you surrender the legal battle for money, custody, possessions, and so forth? Many women have incurred enormous legal bills, lost their homes, and had to declare bankruptcy due to battling within the justice system. Of course, in addition to their tangible cost, extensive court battles are emotionally traumatic for everyone and inevitably injure children when they are involved. The answer to when to stop fighting lies in knowing: knowing how the court is likely to act based on similar cases, knowing what role your fears play in the struggle, and knowing where to draw the line between what you may potentially gain by remaining in the contest and what you are losing each day by not letting go and moving toward your future.

Finding and Using That Fighting Spirit within You

When you hold on to the past, your energy is static, not moving, immobile. You are stuck to one spot on your journey and lack the momentum that is necessary to be creative and step forward. To move beyond divorce you need stamina, strength, and a driving energy that has movement, vibrancy, and determination. Think of yourself as being on one end of the tug-of-war rope. You want to tug and pull your dreams, your passions, and your desires into the future. Are you going to let the disappointments of the past pull you backward? Are you going to allow the ending of your marriage to also mean the ending of all that you hoped would occur in your life as you grew older? Are you going to let this setback stop your desire for love, fulfillment, and joy? Moving ahead, claiming the right to create the most wonderful, exciting, pleasurable life, requires a fighting spirit, a resolve deep within your being that yells, "My life isn't over yet!"

Remember a time when you really went after something important to you. A time when you had made up your mind that nothing was going to stop you from proving your point and making something happen. What did that time feel like? Where in your body did you feel your passion and resolve? What do you recall saying to yourself over and over again that kept you going? Journal about such times in your life. If you do not remember times like this, see if you can imagine what an Olympic athlete must think about just before she or he starts a competition; or the passion that a politician must gather within herself or himself to make the speeches and participate in the debates. This is the stance that you must take right now. You must be willing to fight, drive, and reach toward your future as if your life depended on it, and it does! To state your choice in dramatic words: You can die with your marriage or you can elect to live, dance, and thrive. If you are willing to believe that life is full of possibilities waiting to be uncovered, and that your task—with help, support and determination—is to turn the potential of your life into realities, then you are more than halfway there.

Tips to Creating Powerful Energy

Many women have not had experience creating the kind of powerful energy needed to move through fear. Most women have not created a lofty, long-term vision that required will, drive, and stamina to bring into reality. Whereas more men than women are encouraged to compete through sports and "fight" for what they want, women are usually taught to be subdued, be more collaborative than competitive, and avoid "fighting" at all costs (although fortunately with each generation this changes more and more). The challenge that awaits you is difficult and perhaps new and unfamiliar. But you can do it. Then, once you have successfully taken steps toward transforming your life, you will realize you have a strength that you may not have known you possess. This new capability will serve you and give you confidence for the rest of your life. What a gift!

Below are some guidelines about how to create the energy that you need to leave the past behind and propel yourself to a new piece of your journey.

Don't Make Comparisons

Don't compare your life now as an independent woman with the best times in your marriage or how you hope it will be when you find your ideal mate, if that is your desire. Comparisons force a type of thinking in which one scenario has to be better or worse than another. Living as an independent woman is different from being in a relationship. There will be elements of both circumstances that are wonderful as well as not as ideal. Keep each element of your life separate in your mind so that you can be free to appreciate the best of what each moment has to offer to you.

Move Ahead Step-by-Step

Imagine moving ahead in terms of stepping-stones, not one huge leap. Success begets success. Each activity will bring you closer to your ultimate vision. Maria, an inspiring divorced woman, makes herself do something every day, no matter how small, that will take her closer to her goal. "Even just going to the store and buying stamps," she explained, "is a gain. If I didn't have the stamps, I couldn't send out my resumes. If I didn't send out my resumes, I couldn't get the job. So, if I just get out of bed and purchase the stamps, I have taken an important step." Every action counts. Every action keeps the flow of your energy moving. Movement takes you away from the past and into an exciting future.

Set Limits on Misery

Set limits on the time that you allow yourself to be miserable; however, make sure that you give yourself time and space to feel down, sad, or discouraged. Just as success begets success, misery can beget more misery. Be mindful of how much you allow yourself to indulge in feeling sad or angry about your present circumstances. Everyone "takes to the bed" at times and feels depressed. These moments, in fact, are not only normal, but also important. Judith Duerk, in her book *Circle of Stones,* suggests a very powerful concept about the importance of depression: "Depression comes as a gift forcing one to listen to the voice of the Self within" (1990, 31).

Too much time spent within, however, keeps you from creating a new existence outside of internal reality. It is therefore important that you watch the balance between retreating into sadness and springing into excitement. When you feel a wave of despair coming on, be conscious of setting a time limit on the amount of attention you will give to your grief, unless it is following an immediate loss. Set aside a Sunday to feel sad, eat chocolate, watch movies, and cry. Allow yourself to engage in this important indulgence. But also, plan an activity that will help you return to your journey ahead. For example, on Monday, schedule a walk and a healthy breakfast. Make sure you begin your activities doing something that you enjoy. This will help you to turn your sights outward and tune your energy level so you can get going.

Rely on Yourself to Feel Better

Monitor the tendencies within you that wish for someone else to make you feel better. Having to take care of yourself can become tedious and tiring. The desire to be pampered or spoiled, or just simply have someone take a piece of the load is normal. You become stuck when the wish to have someone else's help turns into you feeling victimized by your situation. The unconscious mind hears the phrase, "I can't stand it any more," and acts literally—it stops standing and walking forward and it "sits" down with a heavy thud. All momentum toward the future is thwarted. To climb out of this pit, ask yourself: "What can I do for myself right now to feel just a little bit better?" Ask this question as if you were taking care of a friend and sincerely wanted to help. In your journal, make a list of actions you can take that will bring a smile to your face. Some suggestions include

♦ Take yourself out for a meal.

♦ Make yourself a nice breakfast, put it on a tray, and eat it in bed.

♦ Buy yourself flowers.

♦ Read a light novel or magazine.

♦ Draw a bath with bath crystals and candles.

Be careful not to compare this act of self-nurturing with the joy of being surprised with a luxurious gift delivered by someone else. Every time you are able to take care of yourself you become stronger and more powerful. Think of it this way: If you can become very effective at attending to your own needs and becoming your own best caretaker, then you can be given gifts and nurturing any time you want it—no wishing, no waiting. And then, when you receive it from an outside source, well, it is icing on the cake!

Ask for Support When You Need It

Sometimes the journey is lonely, confusing, and difficult. You may feel that you don't have any more energy within you to fight. You feel as if you are being pulled back into the pit of misery. During these times it is important to ask for support. No one gets a special medal for making this challenging transformation on her own. During a moment when you are feeling energized, make a list of people and resources you can contact when you need some reinforcement. This support system does not have to consist of best friends or family. Sometimes strangers may give you the strongest boost. Here is a list of community resources that other divorced women have said are helpful:

♦ Family—even members with whom you have not been in touch for a while. Caution—try to stay clear of your former spouse's family.

♦ Friends—when was the last time you contacted a high school friend or old college roommate?

- Religious leaders—even ones you do not know. Needing support may give you the "excuse" you want to seek out spiritual counsel.

- Personal trainers—go check out a gym.

- Beauticians.

- Twelve-step groups.

- Volunteer organizations.

- Hotlines.

- Neighbors.

- Parents of your children's friends.

- Parents Without Partners.

- Weight Watchers.

- Support or social groups.

The key is to let people know when you are down. You do not have to ask for advice or counsel; instead, seek companionship, camaraderie, conversation, and connection. Positive input from another person may be just the energetic ingredient that you need to keep your momentum alive and to prevent you from sliding back into fearful thoughts. Sometimes it is hard to find the motivation to even call someone. In anticipation of this happening (and it does happen to most women at some time during this journey), write yourself a note and place it in a prominent place. Write something like, "Dear Karen, I know you feel empty, lost, and depleted right now. Reach out to someone—you WILL feel better!" This may be the reminder that you need. Making that last big push to hold on to your positive energy affirms your intention to move ahead with your life. The act of affirming what is important to you will significantly help you keep going. More about affirmations will be addressed at the end of this chapter.

Use Anger As Motivation

Anger is a great motivator. Use it! If you learn how to access them powerfully, all emotions can be fuel for forward momentum. Imagine yourself being held captive by a monster. You are standing up, there is a rope around your waist, and this huge, strong monster is pulling you toward him and his dark dirty cave. Go deep inside of yourself and find the voice within you that insists that you do not go and live your life in a musty cave that is filled with spiders. (The more dramatic your images the better.)

What would you say? Would you cry and say, "No, please mister monster, do not do this terrible thing." That probably would not make an impact on the giant. Go inside yourself and find your will to fight. If you were fighting for your life, what would you say? What words would capture your venom, your rage, your fury with a being who wanted to keep you from living your life the way you want? Find a fighting spirit inside yourself. This is the energy that you will need to use when you are feeling stuck. One woman said, "Any time I start feeling sorry for myself I imagine that my ex is in front of me and I say, 'Listen you jerk, you ruined these last five years and I am not going to let you ruin any more.' That motivates me to get out of the house and do something new. I hate being angry, but it sure gets me going."

As discussed earlier in this chapter, beneath the anger you may find some grief and fear that may stymie your energy. The key to using your anger is to allow it to help you fight for the wonderful life that is waiting for you on the other side of this transformative transition. Try watching one of the *Rocky* movies, or listening to one of the theme songs from an upbeat movie like *Flashdance*. Let your anger "psyche you up" into focusing your efforts. Don't be pulled in by the monster. Get tough. Get determined. Destroy any connection that binds you to the negative past and use the energy that you find to launch you ahead.

Treat Yourself with Compassion and Kindness

Remember that the journey of venturing into the future independently is difficult and new. You probably have not done something like this before. Be patient with yourself. When you attempt a new activity that doesn't turn out as you had hoped, say something encouraging to yourself. Many women have developed the destructive habit of criticizing themselves, belittling their efforts, and harshly judging their actions and their products. Transformation consists of millions of small shifts in personality. It takes a long time to learn how to identify people who will be good friends, develop the skills that will enable you to live on your own, and think through the various issues that will help you create a productive and successful independent life. There will be failures. Treat these discouraging moments as learning experiences, and you'll maintain your forward momentum.

Develop a Stubborn Nature about Reaching Your Dreams

Being relentless about reaching your vision allows you to hold on to the energy that will sustain your transformation. There will be many bumps in the road, many moments when the details of living don't seem to be working out. It may be the difficulties of finalizing your divorce settlement, or last-minute changes in your divorce agreement. Your bank may refuse to give you a mortgage if you apply on your own. You may try dating and find yourself meeting men who fall short of the criteria for a mate that you had in mind. Keeping your vision in front of you and refusing to let go of the belief that you can and will create a wonderful new life will keep your forward energy flowing. People around you may disagree with the kinds of changes that you want to make. They may tell you that they "miss the old you." What they have to say may be important feedback; however, in the end, you must commit to staying on the course that you believe is right for you. Do not abandon your vision. Imagine yourself wearing a T-shirt that says: "I am a stubborn woman. I *will* turn my dreams into my reality."

Listen to Your Heart

Listen to your heart: it holds your most cherished dreams, wants, and visions. It will encourage you on those difficult days when you don't want to get out of bed; it will send you words of self-love when you are tempted to blame yourself for all that seems to be going wrong; it will remind you of the beauty that life has to offer and help you listen to the call of oceans, laughter, and music. When the circumstances in life feel cold and rejecting, it is difficult not to internalize all of that pain. Many women find themselves mimicking these negative experiences as they speak to themselves and, as a result, their journey toward transformation stops. When you feel as if this quest is impossible, take a break and spend some quiet time with yourself. Imagine a beautiful wise woman or guardian angel facing you, taking both of your hands in hers, and gazing at you deeply, gently, lovingly. Allow this image, the vision of the energy within your heart, to fill you with love for yourself and all that you are trying to hard to accomplish. Transformation, moving ahead with your life while you also maintain energy for your everyday existence, is difficult. Let the image of a beautiful guide affirm your efforts and help you take the next small steps toward all the joy that you deserve. Allow your heart to be the voice in the darkness that reminds you that you are beautiful, you are wonderful, and you are worthy of living your dreams.

Consider Hiring a Divorce Coach

It is hard to know what you don't know, and it's often hard to vision, plan, and act on your own. Hiring a divorce coach can be very helpful. Divorce coaching is a very special relationship where you are supported and encouraged to create a vision, develop a strategy that leads you in a powerful direction, and, one small step at a time, take action to reclaim your most treasured dreams. A coach is a combination of a personal athletic trainer, therapist, business consultant, and friend whose focus is all on you and helping you get the results that you want. A divorce coach will help you confront the blocks that keep you from transforming and overcome the obstacles that keep getting in your way.

Coaching is not a process of exploring your past and delving into your pain; rather, it is a way to have a partner who is committed to helping you create a new life in the future. A divorce coach will ask you powerful questions, challenge you to consider new ways of confronting old problems, and hold you accountable to take the action steps that you say are necessary to move into your future. Work with a coach will involve that you do a lot of planning, brainstorming, and celebrating. You will be helped to create and hold the energy that will move you beyond the pain of the past and into the future where there are unlimited possibilities. Working with a divorce coach will ensure that you do not walk this journey alone and that you hold your vision with the strength necessary to reclaim your dreams.

Tools to Keep Your Energy Going

Research has proven that the more people envision their goals, and see them in the mind's eye as if they are current reality, the more the body's complex neurological system arranges itself to support actions toward these images (Goleman, Boyatzis, and McKee 2002). The best example of individuals who successfully and constantly use similar tools are elite athletes. Before Olympic gymnasts compete, they mentally rehearse their various routines over and over again in their heads. Downhill ski racers visualize themselves moving down the course, attacking each turn and bump with the utmost precision. Divers envision their dives and feel each bend and twist that their bodies must make before entering the water. Actors, singers, and dancers also utilize mental rehearsal techniques before going on stage. The power of mentally seeing occurring what you want to actually happen is tremendous. (Envisioning negative consequences can also impact your actions.) Here are two ways to help yourself "see and hear" the future.

Collages

You can help yourself imagine your future by collecting pictures from magazines of individuals living the kind of life that you would like to live. For several years, in January a group of women have gathered together to make "New Year's collages." Each contributes a stack of magazines and, together, they spend about an hour ripping out pictures, words, and images that capture what they hope to accomplish in the next year. It's most effective to flip through magazines very quickly—don't think—and tear out images that just call to you. There does not have to be a clear reason for your choices. This allows your unconscious or soul to be a part of the activity. After about an hour, go through your pile, trim the pictures that you have chosen, and glue them in random fashion around a large piece of poster paper. Again, when pasting, try to be as spontaneous as you can—leave thinking out of this activity until the end.

When you have glued everything, put your collage in a place where you can stand back and see it from a distance. Notice the colors that you have chosen, the content of the pictures and words, and the placement of the various images. Do you notice a theme, an emphasis, or a message?

Post this picture in a prominent part of your house. Looking at it each day it will be a reminder of the direction in which you want to be heading. When your energy for moving forward feels low, spending time with the images of this poster will help you reconnect with the reasons why you are working as hard as you are—this poster is your life, the life that you will be living if you keep on your track. Every action you take is a step toward becoming a part of your collage.

Affirmations

Affirmations are short, clear, statements that you say to yourself on a daily basis, the more often the better, which connect you with the successful attainment of your transformation. As with seeing images of your dreams, affirmations assert the direction that you are heading and program the brain to support your actions.

Develop three to five positive statements. Try to memorize them and say them aloud often. Here are some guidelines:

1. Make each affirmation short, no more than ten words.

2. Each affirmation should be written as if it already has occurred. For example, "I am happily living in a condominium by the water."

3. All affirmations are positive; do not use any "nos" or "nots."

4. All are simple statements; do not use any "ands." For example, "All my debts have been paid" or "I maintain a healthy body."

These affirmations are not magic. In themselves, they do not cause your life to be different. They create a framework for what you intend to create in your life. They remind you about what is important to you, what you are working toward, and to what end so much of your creative energy is being expended. What you envision and what you affirm creates the positive, forward-moving energy that you need to drive ahead into your future.

You can create the life that you have always wanted. Your divorce has taught you some valuable lessons. This transition time is giving you the space to contemplate, adjust your sights and direction, and leap ahead into a life that is more possible now than ever.

Chapter 8

Constructing a Transformative Plan

With a vision and energy by your side you may find yourself feeling overwhelmed and skeptical. You may be thinking, "This is too much, too big, too impossible." Or, you may be psyched up and ready to hit your path running. In either case STOP. One of the most prevalent reasons why people don't reach their dreams is because of inadequate planning. For example, how many times have you woken up on a Monday morning and felt ready and committed to diet, only to open the refrigerator and realize that you don't have any of the healthy foods that you need to be successful.

Transforming your life and embracing the unlimited possibilities that exist in the world takes time, patience, persistence, determination, and planning. Transformation is doable. Success begins with a vision, continues with a well-thought-out plan, and moves to reality with directed action.

Developing a complete, organized strategy is key, especially when your dreams involve a long-term goal. You will, in fact, need a step-by-step guide that will involve detailing actions, resources, interim steps, skills that you may have to develop, support systems, decisions that must be made, a timeline that includes points of evaluation and adjustment, and a commitment to staying the course. This chapter provides you with a basic, clear, and linear planning method to take you from one point to the next.

Turning Visions into Goals: A Transformative Exercise

Return to your visions of each of the Pillars. By this time you have created a detailed picture of your dream for each component of your life. To breathe lots of positive energy into your visions, you may have made a collage of images that depict your future, collected objects that symbolize your vision, or spent time imagining the wonderful life that you intend to create. Remember, the more you can actively bring your vision of the future into your life, the more motivated you will be to take action and make your dreams your reality.

Powerful plans are like recipes. They are step-by-step instructions about what to do, when to do it, how to proceed, and the ingredients you need. When you are baking a complex gourmet meal you need to have a list of each dish that you want to prepare and serve. The same is true when transforming your life—you need to have a list of each goal that you want to create. Each one must be clear and understandable so that you can have a clear image to guide you.

In your journal, on the pages designated for each pillar, make a list of the goals that comprise your level-15 visions. For example on the Hobbies and Interests Pillar page you might list

- ♦ Play tennis three times per week with advanced players.

- ♦ Have a fully operational pottery studio in my home.

- ♦ Be a soloist in the church choir.

Remember that these goals are your dreams. You do not have to have the means, skills, or knowledge to bring them about right now. For example, in the above list you may currently be a beginner tennis player, but your vision is to be really good and play three times per week with advanced players. Creating a list of your transformational goals is a crucial beginning to making profound, deep life change.

S-M-A-R-T Planning

Constructing a plan that provides the best possible guidance is based on the development of crystal clear goals. Use the S-M-A-R-T test to fine-tune each of your goals. Make sure each is specific, measurable, realistic, and timely.

Specific

Be specific. What does each goal look like? If a video camera could see the goal, what would be recorded? For example, a goal of "spending time with women friends" is more specific than "finding women who like me." *Liking* is not specific; *spending time,* while a bit nebulous, is a behavior that can be observed.

Measurable

Is the goal countable? How will you know that the goal has been achieved? You want to be able to quantify your goals. Using the example above, a goal of "I will have lunch with one woman friend per week," is more measurable (and a clearer goal) than a goal that merely says "spending time with women friends." A great initial goal might include having one contact with one woman friend per week. The next week or month you might want to expand your goal to include two one-on-one contacts with women friends per week. Your ultimate goal may be to have a large community of women whom you interact with on a daily basis.

Achievable

Can the goal actually happen? Is it achievable? Can someone accomplish the goal in the best of circumstances? Continuing with the above example, wanting to intimately be acquainted with everyone in the state of New York is not achievable. Wanting to be a part of a community of two hundred women all over the state of New York with whom you have at least one verbal exchange over the span of two years may be more achievable.

Realistic

Can your goal be reached given your circumstances? If you are a busy single mother who has three children, has a full-time job out of the home, and is pursuing a college degree, you may be too busy, at this time in your life, to pursue our sample goal. If you are this busy, it might be more realistic to work toward having several comfortable telephone contacts each week with women.

Timely

Can your goal be reached in the time you have allocated? For example, maybe you can be a single mother who has three children, has a full-time job out of the home, is pursuing a college degree, and will reach your goal of having at least one verbal exchange with two hundred women all over the state of New York, as long as you give yourself seven years to accomplish it.

It is helpful to have someone else review your goals with the S-M-A-R-T criteria in mind. This will maximize your possibility of success, as your strategy will be based on sound, clear, doable intentions.

Developing Stepping-Stones

Success begets success. That's the rule when developing a plan of action. Therefore it's vitally important that your strategy be made up of intermediary goals. It should include points of inquiry where you can (1) stop, (2) check in with yourself, (3) notice the actions that you have taken that have increased your satisfaction, and (4) celebrate your progress.

Return to the Pillars Exercise in your journal. Remember that each pillar is comprised of 10 levels of satisfaction. (Level 15 was a tool to help you expand what a fabulous 10 would look like.) Level 10 is your dream. Each numerical level that approaches 10 represents increasing levels of satisfaction with that particular pillar. The next step is challenging. You may want to solicit the input of a friend, support group, or coach. Your job is to set goals that characterize each level of satisfaction above the one you currently are on. Each level that progresses toward your ultimate dream is a *stepping-stone*. More precisely, they are discrete moments in time that mark measurable clear progress toward your vision. Remember to use the S-M-A-R-T model when describing each stepping-stone. Here is an example:

Francine's Story

Francine had been a successful nurse for twenty years. She was a well-respected supervisor who had standing offers to work at many of the local hospitals. At age forty-five, she found herself divorced, with a seventeen-year-old daughter. In addition, Francine was sixty pounds overweight and bored. Over the years, she had grown apart from her family and had no close friends. She felt depressed, alone, and hopeless. When Francine filled out the Pillars Exercise, she gave her Home Environment a 4 ("I don't want to have to mow the lawn and keep up a big house any more"); Physical Body a 1 ("Well, I have one"); Spiritual Life a 0 ("I don't do anything spiritual"); Personal Time a 3 ("All I do is work, go to my daughter's soccer games, sleep, and eat"); Financial Wellness a 7 ("I make good money, but I wish I had some savings and a bigger retirement"); Family a 5 ("My daughter and I are sort of close, but I don't talk to other family members"); Former Spouse a 7 ("He still bugs me, but I don't really care any more"); Friends a 2 ("I've been so busy working I haven't had time for many friends"); Self-Knowledge a 3 ("I don't even know what there is of me to know"); Independence an 8 ("I am OK on my own, but I am pretty lonely"); Career a 5 ("I have a good career, but I don't know if I want to do it forever"); Hobbies and Interests a 2 ("I like soccer, but I don't have any hobbies"); and Intimate Relationships a 0 ("I can't even imagine being intimate again").

Next, Francine wrote out her dreams for each Pillar. This took a bit of time to complete, as she often felt blocked and unable to imagine a future. If this happens to you don't despair; this is normal. When you get stuck, take a break and talk to an encouraging person. Always keep in mind that you have what it takes to create a new life—and that it happens one step at a time. You can do this: patience, confidence, and desire are your tools!

Francine talked extensively with her divorce coach about her hobbies, which she had rated a 2. When she explored what kind of hobbies she had and wished she had pursued as a child, a flicker of excitement came to her face. "I always wanted to go into architecture, but only felt capable of going to nursing school after high school," she said. "If I could do anything," she admitted hesitantly, "I would own a company that restored old buildings." With this vision as a 10 she began to construct stepping-stones in the Career area. At level 5.5 she was going to attend a local community college and take one class. At 6.0 she was doing well in the class. At level 7, she was pursing an architecture associate's degree in college. At level 8, she was earning a bachelor's of science degree in architecture at a four-year college. At level 9, she received her master's degree in architecture. Level 10 was "working as a board-certified architect." She made note of further steps in her dream, like redesigning famous buildings and being known as a creative, talented architect, but placed those to the side for now.

Francine is a great example of reclaiming your childhood dreams by developing a vision and planning stepping-stones. You can also apply this method to current employment. Francine, for example, acknowledged that she could move her current career in directions that would make her feel more satisfied. Her possibilities included changing hospitals, consulting, and working for a local architect to see if she really enjoyed the work. She placed these ideas among her stepping-stones, which allowed her to obtain a thorough vision of what each level of career satisfaction would feel like.

The job in front of you is to fill in each level of your Pillars. You might want to use a separate piece of paper for each Pillar and leave plenty of space to add ideas to each stepping-stone as your imagination expands. Again, working with a few friends, a support group, or a coach will provide you the opportunity for additional input. This exercise will be a lot of fun as you allow your thoughts to run wild. Reclaiming old dreams is like connecting with old friends—there is a lot of catching up to do and you will remember why you enjoyed them so much. Fight any impulses to dampen your enthusiasm. Your life will not be judged by anyone based on your progression toward your aspirations. The value of working toward your most sacred desires is immense. Dreams can come true, especially when you actively create the mechanisms for making them happen.

Constructing a Planning Board

A planning board will be your road map. On your board will be your goals, stepping-stones, and actions. There are many different ways to construct this board. A favorite is to spread a very large piece of mural paper across an empty wall. Make a long horizontal line for each of the thirteen pillars. At the far right side of each line write down and draw a circle around one, two, or three words that capture the essence of your ultimate vision. On the far left side of each line, write the level of satisfaction that you are currently experiencing with each Pillar. Next, divide each line and place a small circle for each stepping-stone that you will need to pass as you work toward your vision. It's as if the line represents a road that you are traveling left to right. It does not matter if each line has different numbers and different spacing.

The intention of your planning board is to track your progress from where you are now, to the circumstances in your life in which you will feel bliss. If you can, place target dates by each stepping-stone. At the least, write down today's date and the target date of when you would like to arrive at your destination. You will probably not know the date for each stepping-stone; however, it might be helpful to place a target date by the stepping-stone that comes next, after today. You might decide that you don't want to work on some of these areas right away, so the dates that you place will be quite distant in the future. Remember, stay realistic (the "R" in S-M-A-R-T) and take your life circumstances into account when you set dates. For example, you may decide that you do not want to try dating until your children move away from home, or that it would be better for you to pursue a fitness plan during a less stressful time in your life. These are fine decisions and reflect sound planning. Place *working dates,* dates that make sense right now, on the first stepping-stone of each pillar. (If you are at a level 5 right now, place a target date for when you would like to be at level 6, and so forth.)

There are other formats that people find more useful for their planning board. Some women prefer having one piece of 8½ x 11 paper for each Pillar. They post on their walls only the Pillars on which they are actively working. Other women make a notebook where they have a section dedicated to each Pillar. In each of these alternative formats, the individuals still use a horizontal line to represent their path.

It is important that you use whatever organization tool will keep your journey moving forward, clear, and alive. The more your planning board is actually visible so that you can see it on a daily basis, the more likely it is that it will become a conscious part of your daily thoughts and activities.

Brainstorming Actions

Stepping-stones mark your progression. *Actions* are the behaviors that will move you forward. To complete your planning board and have the strategy and clarity that will form the map for your transformation, it is necessary for you to brainstorm the hundreds of small, discrete actions that you will need to take to reach each stepping-stone. It is difficult to think of everything that you will need to know or do to reach each step along your path. However, the following topics and questions are helpful to explore in the action brainstorming process:

- Research: What do I need to know? What research do I have to do?

- Resources: Who can I contact for information or direction? What are some resources that would help me?

- Logistics: What activities do I need to complete, organize, and so on? What are the logistics involved?

- Possibilities: What are other ways that I could accomplish the same purpose? What are other possibilities?

- Support: What kind of support do I need to make my goal happen?

With these topics and questions and others that you find helpful, it is time to brainstorm all of the actions you need to take to complete each step. Pads of small sticky notes are an ideal tool to help you accomplish this task. Start with thinking about one pillar, perhaps the one on which you would like to begin working first. With one pad of notes begin to write down each action that you will need to take to move from one stepping-stone to the next, one action per piece of note paper. Keep in mind the S-M-A-R-T guidelines. It is helpful to imagine yourself working on one of your goals. What do you see yourself doing to complete this goal? Place each of these actions, one at a time, on a sticky note (one action per note).

Allow your creative mind to guide you when you make this list. Try not to become overwhelmed by the number of tasks you generate. Actually, the more details you are able to think about and place on sticky notes, the easier will be your task because you will have thought it through step-by-step.

For example, when Francine was working on her Career Pillar and moving toward taking one class in architecture at a local community college, her actions were as follows

Research (information to gather)

- What community colleges are in my area
- Which schools have an introductory course in architecture
- What times, places, days are the classes offered
- The cost for taking the classes
- If I am academically eligible for the course; are there any pre-requisite classes

Resources (people to call for information, help, ideas)

- Friends or acquaintances who have taken courses at community colleges
- Established architects
- Registrar at the local community colleges

Logistics (actions that need to be completed)

- Change work schedule so that I can attend desired classes
- Overview my daughter's plans so that schedules are complementary
- Get and complete the application for admission
  - Health forms
  - Recommendations
- Get and complete forms for a scholarship
  - Bank statements
  - Tax statements
- Purchase the required textbook
- Obtain a parking permit

Possibilities (places to consider if the community college plan does not work)

- Volunteer with an architect to obtain some on-the-job training
- Consider four-year college options

Support (talk with the following people about how they can best support me)

- ◆ Coach

- ◆ Daughter

- ◆ Classmates

- ◆ On-campus resources

Each of the above items was placed on a sticky note.

When you have thought of all of the actions that you can (feel free to add more as they come to you), spread all of the notes in front of you and arrange them sequentially. What do you need or want to do first? Place them on your planning board in the space between the last goal (stepping-stone) that you accomplished and the one to which you are headed. These are the tasks ahead of you. As you complete the assignment on each note take it off your planning board. Effective ways to take action will be covered in the next chapter.

It's Important to Plan

It is tremendously tempting to either skip or minimize the planning phase in favor of a more spontaneous approach and "just get started." When you do this, however, you risk forgetting an important step. In addition, having some kind of charting and record-keeping procedure will help you stay motivated and energized. You will see your productivity and progress even when the tasks seem rather small. This realization will keep you going and, step-by-step, day-by-day, you will see yourself moving toward dreams and visions you never thought possible. Will you ever get to the end? Is there ever really an end? With each step, more ideas come and your journey continues. Each step you take—no matter how small—is a win. The idea is not how far you get—whether you actually become a multimillionaire, own the dream business or obtain academic degrees. What is most important is that you're empowered to move beyond the past, enjoy the present, and, each day, realize that the strength within you is bringing more and more elements of happiness into your life.

Chapter 9

Taking Action

You have a vision; you have a plan; you have your planning board; and you feel energized and ready. It's now time to roll up your sleeves and take action.

Building on the Past

Most women have set goals and tried to reach them. Whether the target was weight loss, career advancement, wealth, learning a new skill, or a high grade in school, the idea of working toward a special objective is probably familiar. These past experiences hold significant lessons as you make your final preparations to transform your life after divorce. It is helpful to be aware of the strengths and weakness you currently bring to this life-changing time.

A Transformative Exercise

In your journal, recall three to five times in your life where you engaged in visioning, planning, and acting. Write extensively about these occasions, emphasizing everything you did that helped you achieve your goals. In other words, what have you done in the past that has worked? Be as clear and specific as you can. Next, as you record each goal, write about the moments when you felt weak, times when you did not pursue your end by the most effective means possible. What got in the way? What happened to stop your progress forward? If you did not reach your desired outcome, what blocked you? If you are unable to answer these questions, you might want to seek some insight from guides in your life such as friends, family, your coach, or a therapist. Hold off taking new actions until you have gained clarity both about your skills as well as your past stumbling points. Your stamina to move through challenges and your ability to succeed will be enhanced by understanding past experiences. Your strength to follow your current path and pursue new goals increases when you build on past successes and use techniques that worked for you before.

People tend to be creatures of habit, repeating behaviors unless a new consciousness is created. Robert Fritz (1984) called this phenomenon "the path of least resistance." To maximize your current intentions, learn from past efforts. When you have journaled and highlighted actions and thoughts that have helped you succeed, as well as those moments that were difficult, make a list of the lessons you need to keep in mind. Fill in the following sentence in your journal: "To succeed this time, I need to remember to. . . ." Rewrite this list on a separate piece of paper and post it in a prominent place next to your planning board. You will be most apt to use these important lessons if they are visible and available to you.

The Commitment to Move Forward

All roads contain some bumps and potholes that are frustrating. "I really want to make the calls to those job ads," a woman said, "but I just can't get myself to do it." She, like others in similar circumstances, was perplexed by her behavior. On the one hand she knew that she wanted to change her life: she really wanted a new job. Yet when it came down to making the telephone calls necessary to begin the job-search process, she couldn't find the motivation to act.

There is a difference between wanting something and having a commitment to a particular action. This is an important distinction that can impact the success of your plan. *Wants* stem from emotions:

they tend to fluctuate and change with time and circumstances. They may reflect trends, styles, popular opinion, or mood. Even your most passionate wants can be nebulous, making it difficult to know exactly why you want or don't want something. *Commitments,* on the other hand, are the most fundamental parts of who you are. They are your values, your ideals, the guiding principles that define the directions of your life. Commitments are foundational parts of the personality.

Goals that are based on wants or preferences tend to be easy to abandon. Actions that are based upon fundamental commitments have a lasting vitality. People are driven to engage in actions that reflect their commitments, as these deeds are consistent with their overall life direction and purpose. Understanding how your goals and plans fit with your major life commitments will provide you a powerful context for your transformational journey. It will provide meaning, purpose, and mission to all that you aim to do. When you act in accordance with your commitments, the following phrase will describe your *preaction attitude:* "These actions are so important to me that I am willing to do whatever it takes to make them happen. I am absolutely and completely committed to engaging in the plan that I have created and to claiming my visions because completing this journey will allow me to live the life I want to live and become the person that I passionately want to be."

Commitment requires that you know what you value. Most people take their values for granted and have difficulty articulating them. Robert Fritz observes that people's "fundamental choices" (values) are usually "to be free, to be healthy, and to be true to oneself" (1984, 190). While these are certainly important attributes, women often articulate them slightly differently:

- ◆ Financial freedom and independence
- ◆ Loving, deep partnership
- ◆ A healthy, vibrant mind and body
- ◆ A comfortable lifestyle, including travel and a lovely home
- ◆ A close, supportive family
- ◆ Intellectual and cultural opportunities
- ◆ The pursuit of a spiritual path
- ◆ Involvement in a supportive community
- ◆ Stature

♦ Service to the greater world community

♦ And more . . .

Values Identification: A Transformative Exercise

In your journal, identify four to six of your most important, fundamental values—those ideals, concepts, and pursuits that are extremely important to you. Spend time writing about each of these areas: describe your definition of each notion and write why each one is important to you. You might include how you came to value a certain perspective and how it has impacted your life. Next, go back to your action plan and, above each vision, write down the value that is connected it. For example, if one of your visions is to earn an advanced degree in college, you might write the following: "I want to earn an advanced college degree because with this knowledge I will be able to train teachers who will work in third-world countries. This is a part of my commitment to making a difference in the world."

A forty-year-old woman illuminated the importance of these connections. She wanted to start a business and make it very economically successful. However, week after week she found herself not having the time to take the actions necessary to bring her dream business into reality. She spoke passionately about wanting to create this business. She also expressed great frustration at not pursuing this desire. Interestingly, this woman suffered from an extreme form of diabetes. She was diligent at making sure that she exercised, followed her diet, and learned about the latest discoveries that might help her cope with this illness. Why she was able to be so attentive to the pursuit of her health and not to the development of her business? She explained, as if it should be obvious, "Well, one is life and death and the other is 'just' business." (Her use of the word "just" is a clue that she wasn't approaching her business dream in a very powerful way.)

What made the life and death issue so compelling to her was that she wanted to "live a long life," which is a fundamental commitment. When she connected the two, she realized that creating a large successful business was also one of her fundamental commitments, a piece of something very important to her: financial success. She said that financial success will allow her to stand on her own two feet, provide for her children, and grow old without being afraid—three goals to which she is absolutely committed so that she will be secure in her independence.

Realizing how her plan of action was a behavioral expression of an attribute that was sacred to her—the value of independence—and not "just" an activity, elevated the importance of her plan. Just as she was dedicated to pursuing a healthy lifestyle that would keep her diabetes in check and allow her to live a long life, she became equally attentive to bringing her vision of a successful business into the world. Her weekly goals became easy to complete. When she felt blocked, she reminded herself about why she was doing what she was doing and thus felt renewed, purposeful, and reenergized.

With your commitments clear and in front of you, your actions will flow. In the book *Changing for Good* the authors state that: "The very act of committing yourself to a given alternative increases the likelihood of success. The more entirely you throw yourself into a new way of behaving, the more likely you are to experience that way as being the best path to follow. In any case, commitment requires you to have faith in your ability to succeed at the action you have chosen to take" (Prochaska, Norcross, and DiClemente 1994, 154).

During this period of transition, revisiting your commitments and affirming what is important to you will strengthen your dedication to your transformational journey and deepen your resolve to take the actions that will bring you profound change. With this sense of mission and meaning, you will be able to carry out your various plans and have the tools you need to move ahead.

Approaching Action

It is time to walk to the end of the diving board and confidently dive into the water. The metaphor of diving off a springboard accurately describes your final challenge: you must make a strong, well-calculated approach to the task at hand, execute the twists and turns required of a well-coordinated effort, and, finally, plunge headfirst, with elegance and minimal splash, toward the next stage of your life. The activity is complex and at the same time very manageable, especially with the utilization of several well-established tools.

Keep Your Actions Small

Keeping your actions small is instrumental in helping you succeed. Small actions feel doable. They are approached with an optimistic expectation of completion. Conceptualize all actions as a sequence of small, basic behaviors. For example, writing a letter involves (1) acquiring the appropriate stationery; (2) thinking through the content of each portion of the letter; (3) writing the letter; (4) editing the letter; (5) printing the letter; (6) confirming the address of the recipient(s); (7) purchasing stamps; (8) mailing the letter. On days that you feel energetic, you could complete a project, such as the above, during one afternoon. On days that you feel tired and pessimistic, just take one mini-step. At the least, you go to bed one action closer to your vision than when you woke up in the morning. A small-step approach gives you flexibility and choice, and makes it possible for momentum to develop. When you respect the fluctuations in your capacity to make changes, you can sustain the pace of your journey. A journey begins with the first step and continues one small step at a time until you reach your destination, or at least a satisfying place to rest for a while.

Slow and Steady Wins the Race

Remember the childhood story of the tortoise and the hare? This is the tale of a race between the speedy rabbit and the poky turtle. The rabbit started out strong, became tired, and was unable to complete the course. The turtle, on the other hand, took her time, ambled along the path, and made it successfully to the end. The possibility of transforming one's life and leaving the unsatisfactory elements of a marriage behind is both difficult and exciting. One woman said, "I just want it to be the future right now." When the pain of the ending subsides, it is tempting to leap onto the path like the hare and sprint toward the future, progressing as quickly as possible. The problem with this approach is that quick-start success may seduce you to start to change your life at a speed that you cannot maintain. Thus, you risk becoming tired, frustrated, and discouraged with your plan over the long haul.

It's wiser to implement a slow-and-steady approach to your actions. Do not be tempted to alter everything at one time, in one week, one month, or even one year. Refer to your plan often. Assign time goals to your actions that allow you to make a shift in your life, live with it for a while, and then engage in another action. Use the levels of each pillar to mark your progress. Observe the pace with which you move toward your level-10 ideal. Rapid progress may signal growth that will not last. An apt equivalent is weight loss: diets that enable you to drop "twenty pounds in twenty days" also cause you to gain twenty pounds in the next twenty days (or even less time). Small steps, taken at a slow, deliberate, well-conceived pace will bring about change that can last.

Set Weekly Goals

Your life is probably very busy both logistically and emotionally. It is therefore easy to let your plan for transformation slip out of your consciousness. Continual steady movement will help your morale. Experiencing small changes in your life provides hope and allows you to feel optimistic about creating and living the joyful life you want. Schedule a meeting with yourself on Sunday evenings and decide what actions you are going to work on during the week ahead. Plan (1) what you are going to do, (2) when you are going to do it, and (3) how you are going to complete your assignment.

Make specific dates with yourself during the week to complete your tasks. Write these intentions down just as if they were important appointments with a doctor or a friend. The more formal you are about scheduling your tasks, the higher the likelihood is that they will be done. Writing your actions in your weekly calendar gives them a tone of importance; they feel more like priorities (which they are). This will help your motivation and keep you on track. Honor your efforts by keeping the appointments with your action plan. Avoid all temptations to cancel if you "don't feel like it" or if something that sounds more fun comes along. It's better to engage in a smaller step than to cancel a step all together. Creating the habit of working on your transformation plan each week at the same time helps change occur. These actions are about your life. Weekly goals become yearly gains. You can do it by being methodical and determined.

Use Visual Reminders

The expression "out of sight, out of mind" is true, especially when you are busy. The use of visual reminders helps keep your intention to take action in the forefront of your mind. Small, well-placed notes that cue you to make a particular phone call, write an important note, or research a vital resource, will support your momentum. Choose three locations in your day-to-day life that you see the most. These could be your computer, your bedroom mirror, your kitchen table, and so forth. Post reminders of your actions in these places. Use brightly colored paper and large, clear writing. You can think of these notes as your "external brain." When the brain in your skull is overloaded, rely on the posted notes to direct and nudge you to take action. When you complete the assignment, remove the note and toss it away—task completed, congratulations!

Take Time to Review Completed Actions

Periodically review your activities. Debrief yourself about the effectiveness of your plan. Are you moving forward? Are blocks arising that you did not anticipate? Do you sense that you are moving ahead too quickly or too slowly? What kind of adjustments would help you be more comfortable with your plan? Are additional actions needed that you had not thought about before? Reviewing the strategy itself as well as your approach to your plan makes you more effective. It is inevitable that you will learn a lot about yourself as you take action. During this review time, find ways to implement what you have learned.

For example, Arlene was struggling financially. Her former husband didn't always pay his court-ordered child support payments, and he never paid on time. She already owed money to the divorce attorney and she was reticent to add more to this bill, yet she needed legal advice. Feeling desperate, she called a local agency that was connected to the courts. They were happy to field her questions. She learned new ways that she could help herself and, more important, discovered the power of asking questions and not excepting her own sense of helplessness. With the tool of asking questions about things she does not know beside her, Arlene approaches other action steps feeling stronger and wiser. Most actions contain lessons that can be applied to future steps. Taking the time to review your actions reveals new assets and provides new strength for your continued journey.

Reward Yourself Often

All actions taken in pursuit of your life goals deserve recognition. As a child, parents and teachers most likely rewarded you. It is difficult to shift the source of reinforcement from an outside person to yourself. So many women believe that it doesn't count if they have to reward themselves. You're encouraged to change this thinking. The best source of reward is yourself because you know exactly what you want. Others merely guess what would bolster your resolve, and they often guess wrong. Make a list of treats you would like. Allow them to range in scope, cost, and nature from a visit to a favorite locale, a phone call to a distant friend, or a manicure, to exotic travel (for times when you feel especially deserving).

Rewards don't have to be dramatic. A midday nap can be a well-earned gift. A note on your refrigerator that says, "I did it!" is a wonderful method of self-congratulation. Crucial to your continued efforts is recognizing how hard you are working to make your life better. The implementation of your action plan is not easy, especially in those moments when you are exhausted or having to do something that is unfamiliar or uncomfortable.

Many, many women allow themselves to stay stuck in the sadness of their divorce. Some take on the cloak of being a victim, others cannot find the courage to imagine a new life. The fact that you are reading this book and considering ways to move ahead means that you are an open, courageous woman. You are to be honored for each page of this book that you have read and each exercise that you have completed or will complete. Can you honor yourself for these efforts? If you hear a voice within you that says, "Reading is no big deal," challenge this statement. Every step that you take on your own behalf is a big deal. You may recall the stages of change that were discussed in chapter 4. Contemplation is an important step in the change process. Through reading and contemplating, you are taking an action. How will you reward yourself for doing this? When you follow your actions with some sort of reward or self-recognition, your resolve to transform your life will be strengthened and your likelihood for success multiplied.

Taming the Procrastination Monster

The *procrastination monster* traps most people from time to time. These moments are discouraging and can result in a rejection of the entire plan. If you find your progress being halted and feel yourself resistant to taking any action, even a small mini-step, try one of these techniques:

♦ Take a time-out for an hour, a day, a week, even a month, and then return to the plan. Make sure you set limits to the length of this time-out.

- If a particular action feels somewhat uncomfortable, do it right away at the beginning of the day. Recognize that from time to time you will have to make an uncomfortable phone call or fill out a form that reminds you of disappointments. When you find the strength within yourself to "do what has to be done," however, you are proving your ability to meet life's challenges. You are a courageous, capable woman.

- Try the "one-two-three-four-five method": First work for one minute, then take a one-minute break; then work for two minutes and take a two-minute break; then work for three minutes and take a three-minute break, and so on. See if this jump-starts your momentum.

- Alternate between something you do not want to do and something you enjoy doing.

- Remind yourself that procrastination is a normal part of completing an extensive task. You are OK. You are not bad. Give yourself encouragement, take a breath, and try one of the above techniques.

- Journal a dialogue between the part of you that doesn't want to do anything and the part that wants to move forward. Use a different color pen for each voice. Especially try to understand the resistant voice and see what she needs to move forward. Find a way to work with her. Don't bully her. Nurture her. Compromise with her. Partner with her. Think of times someone wants you to do something that you don't want to do. What convinces you to act? Work with your resistances, not against them.

- Remember that the journey of transformation is long. Anticipate that there will be times when you will feel blocked and be prepared to not reject your entire plan. If procrastination lasts for a long period of time it may be useful to ask a coach or support person for help.

Staying Accountable

Accountability is the mechanism for checking in with yourself, or others, and taking stock of how you are doing. Are you progressing at the speed that you want? Are you completing actions on the schedule that you had allotted? Are you attending to all portions of your plan? Are you rewarding yourself? Are you journaling? Are you charting and utilizing all of the different mechanisms that help you take successful actions? Accountability involves record keeping, reflecting, making adjustments, and noting progress. It is a positive process that promotes strength and momentum. It's not an activity that creates shame or blame for not acting in a way that you might prefer.

Similar to the area of reward and reinforcement, you're most likely used to being held accountable by others. "Did you do your homework?" "Did you do the laundry?" So much of the divorce transformation involves learning how to turn inward—to yourself—to develop the independence to act, think, and feel. This is a time to develop a sense of self-accountability, to realize that taking actions that move you toward living a joy-filled, meaningful life involves establishing a very sacred bond with yourself. Each action that moves you ahead strengthens this bond. Holding yourself accountable, therefore, is an important pragmatic and spiritual activity. These occasions for review must be empowering. They are times when you cheer yourself on, feel pride in what you are doing, and make resolutions to take the next step.

An Accountability Ceremony: A Transformative Exercise

You may find that creating an *accountability ceremony* adds an important element of inner strength to the process. Light a candle, say aloud what you intend to do in the next time period, and affirm yourself, your efforts, and your vision. This may seem similar to prayer, or perhaps it feels more like a rally. Whatever approach is best for you, having a continual mechanism for review, self-reporting, and celebration will help assure you that you are taking action. Additionally, it will keep you connected to the overall intention of using this life transition as a powerful time to create deep and lasting change.

The Importance of Support

No single element in the plan is as important as support. Support sustains action. The more varied your sources of support are, the stronger and more capable you will be of taking this journey from start to a finishing point. Having a broad support system is important because your needs differ constantly. Having coffee with a group of women friends may give you a sense of belonging, which supports you during times when you feel scattered and disconnected. Receiving support from a coach may give you the professional direction, guidance, and encouragement you need. A special woman friend may help you express your vulnerability and fears so that you can regroup and regain a sense of strength. Meeting with a divorced women's support group, where other women are going through similar challenges, may reassure you about the normality of your struggles. And, going onto a Web site that focuses on divorce, dating, career issues, single motherhood, and so forth, may offer supportive information that is empowering, clarifying, and rejuvenating.

It may be difficult for you to reach out for support, and yet it is essential that you make these connections. Starting with professional sources—educational, psychological, religious, and so on—may be the easiest place to begin. Each woman needs support in her own unique ways. Therefore, not everyone whom you contact will be the best match for you for this purpose. Some people can support one component of your journey, such as how to approach a particular task, but not be as much of an aide in other areas, such as in the emotional realm. Accept the piece of support that each person is able to give you. No matter how small, it is a gift.

Finally, keep in mind that at the heart of this transformational journey is the quest to become comfortable with being an independent woman. While support from others is important and valuable, the most powerful source of support is that which you are able to provide to yourself. If you are new to acting on your own, this may take a while to cultivate. Keep the goal of developing peace and support within yourself, and utilize the love and encouragement of others as extra springs from which you can drink when your own supplies feel low.

With available support from within and from others, your ability to create and take action will flow and lead you in the direction of unlimited possibilities. Each step, each action, is a success—it is evidence of your commitment to take control of your life and to make it an existence that reflects your innermost longings and callings. Celebrate your actions daily and acknowledge the journey traveled, whether it is extensive or it seems relatively short. Affirm and appreciate yourself, especially on those days when action feels impossible. You, and you alone, are the instrument for change. Step-by-step, day-by-day, transformation is possible. Anatole France said, "To accomplish great things, we must not only act, but also dream, not only plan, but also believe." (Lunden 2001, 32). Believe in yourself; believe in your capacity to succeed. This will light the beacon and empower you to create the actions that make tomorrow wonderful.

The Incredible Journey

Meg leads a support group for divorced women. She shares:

> *I have been where you are, sat where you are sitting, getting ready to begin a new part of life, and yet not sure I wanted to begin at all. I made the decision to ask my husband to leave the house. I knew what I didn't want—a life with an inactive, depressed man. After he moved, I had no idea what I wanted. I was scared and unable to do anything but go to work, come home, and watch television. One night I woke up shaking and sobbing. I wondered if I had made a mistake ending my marriage. I thought about calling my husband first thing in the morning and seeing if we could give it another try (yet again). And then I heard a voice say, "No!" I realized that I could not go back, that even though I didn't know what was ahead, I had power over my future alone. Something shifted within me during that long night. I was still frightened, but I was also energized. The next week, I got a burst of unbounded energy. I painted my kitchen cabinets, enrolled in an accounting class, started walking every morning, and got my hair cut and colored.*
>
> *Now, five years later, I realize that while I was married, my whole personality was stuffed into a very tiny box labeled "wife." I am not sure how this happened, but I do know that all I did was compressed into one, tight, uncreative blob. That night the lid sprung open and I found that there was more to me than I had ever realized. There are things that I want to try, new people I want to meet, places I want to travel. Well, all I can say is that it is incredible.*

Pushing the lid off your box and discovering life's unlimited possibilities and potential are the gifts that await you as you use the event of divorce as a catalyst for transformation. Each Pillar of the exercise at the beginning of this book represents a dimension of your life that awaits exploration. As you consider all of your dreams, you become more aware of the whole, vibrant woman that has been lying dormant within you. While divorce meant the ending of a relationship, it marked the beginning of a transformational journey. And now, having envisioned, planned, acted, persevered, and stayed the course, a new you has arrived and is stronger, wiser, and more capable and expansive. Congratulations. Howl at the moon; a new day has begun!

Chapter 10

Relating to Men Again

Hopefully, you have been inspired to you use your divorce to help you connect with the fullness of who you are as a woman. Reclaiming your dreams, creating a strategy to move forward, and taking action have allowed you to expand the concept of how you think about yourself. Now you have begun to live with a huge, glowing, broad-reaching sense of yourself, your life, and your direction. Attending to the complexity of who you are affirms that you are more than a role, a job, or an expectation. You are a woman with interests and talents reaching out in many directions.

Contemplating and engaging the breadth of your transformation may bring you to decide that having a relationship with a special man is a piece of your vision. If so, it is important to turn your attention to exploring how you want to remake the way that you create intimate male/female relationships.

Transforming the way that you connect to men best begins by reconsidering the role that you want a man to play in your life.

Traditionally, women have been encouraged to make men the center-piece of their existence. You may have been taught: "relationship first, you second." This old-fashioned point of view minimizes the expansive potential that you have as a woman. Additionally, when men occupy this "relationship first" place, the potential for an equal, mutually empowering relationship becomes difficult as the connection is unbalanced. When you become the center of your life, the following changes in your thinking and relating occur:

- ◆ You make sure that there is consistency between your heart's desire and the kind of men you are choosing.

- ◆ You acknowledge male/female differences as equal, alternative "ways."

- ◆ You accept responsibility for taking care of your own needs, and recognize that constructive give-and-take involves exchange that is freely offered.

- ◆ You understand that a lifelong relationship with a man is a partnership that requires compatibility beyond, and including, love.

Transformation occurs by shedding some of your old conceptions. Being open to thinking differently is challenging in that it often initially causes discomfort; however, as has been discussed before, discomfort can be the signal that you are on your growing edge and wonderful transformation is about to occur. Be open to new ways of thinking about yourself and men. Perhaps you will discover parts of yourself that have been hidden thus far.

Reflecting Your Heart's Desire

Find a place where you can be quiet and still. Close your eyes, take some deep breaths, and feel the beating of your heart. Remember times when you have been gloriously happy. These might have been moments when you were in love with a person or times when an experience like a sunset or a particularly beautiful vista elicited feelings of awe within you. In your journal, write down as many feeling words as you can think of that describe your experience of joy, love, and happiness. Make the list long and exhaustive. Your adjectives will likely range and include words such as playful, giddy, gentle, sensual, tender, aware, and passionate.

Now, in your journal, make a second list. This time make a list of adjectives that best describe you when you interact with men. If you want to glean the most from this exercise, ask men with whom you relate in social situations how you come across to them, or ask women friends who have seen you engage with men to describe how they have seen you behave. Compare these lists. How similar are they? It would not be unusual to see two completely different lists.

Women today are challenged more than any generation before to take on a multitude of tasks, roles, and responsibilities. At work you must stay clear, directed, and focused. At home, especially if you are a mother, you must also stay organized, alert, and capable. If you are a student, your mind is occupied with complicated intellectual challenges. Your daily requirements probably do not give you much time to focus on attending to emotions and being playful, gentle, open, inquisitive, and so forth—all of which are expressions more from your heart than your head. When she was engaged in this exercise, Eve, an attorney, said: "I can't be in touch with my emotions or my heart. If I do, my sympathies will complicate the case I am trying to prove!"

The difficulties for women come when, at the core of their being, their hearts, they experience themselves one way ("I really am a fun and nurturing person"), and the qualities they are used to displaying to the world comprise a different, sometimes opposite set of characteristics. Who are you really: the assertive, organized, direct woman, or the romantic, gentle, playful woman? The answer, of course, is both. Understanding the concept of what energies you project—the overall sense of you that is felt by others—will help you answer the question: "Am I really being the person with men that I like best within myself?"

Another way of understanding the dichotomy many women experience between their inner self and their outer behaviors is discussed in Jungian psychology, which differentiates between two sets of qualities: masculine and feminine (Whitmont 1979). Men and women possess both groups of traits. The qualities of organizing, clarity, focus, driving action, and the like have been labeled by Jungian psychologists as *masculine*. Flowing activities, emotional expression, and connection are labeled as *feminine qualities*. David Deida, in his book *Intimate Communion*, creatively describes masculine and feminine attributes by comparing feminine energy to Hawaii, "flowing, open, wild, radiant"; and masculine energy to New York, "goal-oriented, scheduled, directed, focused, self-disciplined" (1995, 21). According to Deida, when you display feminine energy you wear colorful clothes; you are engaging and animated; and your emotions are flowing and dynamic and enliven a conversation. He says that when you are displaying masculine energy you are structured, consumed, black-and-white, and in control.

Refer to the lists that you just journaled. What set of characteristics, masculine or feminine, best describe you when you are feeling happy and loving? What set of characteristics best describe you when you are interacting with men? Gloria had a revelation when she looked at her lists, "My heart is feminine, and yet I tend to be more masculine when I am with men. I decide where we are going to go. I direct conversations. I don't mean this to be a negative thing, but I guess I stay in a 'get down to business' kind of attitude whether I am at work or at play." Following the psychological adage "opposites attract," when Gloria behaves in a masculine way what kinds of men is she likely to attract? Those who are more feminine.

Who Are You Attracting? A Transformative Exercise

Spend some time thinking about the relationships that you have had with men and would like to create with men in the future. Journal your responses to the following:

♦ Describe the traits of the men who tend to seek you out.

♦ Describe the traits of your former husband.

♦ What traits did your former husband possess that you were attracted to at the beginning of your relationship?

♦ What attractive traits did your former husband possess toward the end of your relationship?

♦ Describe the kind of man you think you would like to bring into your life.

As you review your answers, do you notice any patterns? Do the men who are attracted to you possess masculine or feminine traits? (Warning: Do not confuse the word *feminine* with effeminate. Men with feminine traits tend to be expressive, dreamers, spontaneous, and so forth. They are not necessarily female-like in their mannerisms.) Do the men you are attracted to possess any particular set of traits? People tend to be attracted to energy that they do not exhibit, but hold within their unconscious. This is called *projection,* and explains why opposites attract.

If you find that the kind of men you are attracted to tend not to be attracted to you, it may be because there is a difference between the energy of your heart and the way you act. Your more feminine heart calls you to bond with a more masculine man (or vice versa), yet your behaviors (which may display the more masculine traits that you use in your day-to-day existence), are attracting men who possess more feminine energy. If your heart has a feminine essence, you desire a more masculine man, but your more masculine behaviors are, instead, attracting a more feminine man.

As you seek to transform your life and become more empowered to create the relationships and visions that are important to you, it is essential that you make sure that the spirit of who you consider yourself to be is accurately displayed through your image and your actions. Giving yourself permission to try different ways of presenting yourself and noting the response that you receive will help you decide ways that you may want to change to create the intimate relationships that you desire. This is not about changing your behavior to manipulate men, it is about having more options to express the magnitude, depth, and breadth of who you really are so that you can choose the kind of mate you really want. When you are able to personify the essence of who you are—who you feel yourself to be at the core of your being—then you will create intimate relationships that captivate your heart, mind, and spirit. This will open the pathway toward happiness and more successful relationship experiences.

Honoring the Differences between Men and Women

Another male/female perspective is that men and women are different from each other. On one level, this statement is overly simplistic; and yet it is true in some important and fundamental ways. To create true intimacy in male/female relationships, a bridge must be built to connect men and women, despite their differences. This bridge is based on your acknowledgment of the deep, essential similarities between the genders as well as your acceptance of the differences. This allows you to experience life on equal terms as opposed to harboring a hierarchical, critical attitude.

Sometimes the similarities between men and women seem hard to detect. Women speak among themselves about how deficient men are emotionally or how they do not have the skills to maintain relationships. These perceptions come because many women tend to express emotions and relate to others in a particular, female-gender-specific way. However, often men share rather familiar and similar fears and emotions. For example, when a man begins to get to know a woman, he asks himself questions such as these: Will she really understand me? Will she really respect my efforts and who I am? Will she acknowledge my pain, struggles, and challenges as equal to hers? The vulnerability that many men experience has caused them to distance themselves and their hearts from women, and thus made the creation of intimate connections difficult. One man said, "Women think they are the only ones who do not feel safe on dates. We don't either!"

To establish meaningful relationships with men, it is essential that women be open to seeing parts of men's psyches that they had thought did not exist. It would also be helpful to realize that men may (and do) possess similar thoughts and feelings, but they often express and experience them differently than women. This creates the potential for deeper connection. It removes stereotypical thinking that blocks your ability to see men individually and it opens the pathway for more meaningful, intimate knowing. The awareness that both genders experience vulnerabilities, both genders experience powerlessness, and both genders experience themselves as victims of circumstance from time to time—although each gender may express and experience it differently—is a great way to begin creating intimacy with men. Embracing the reality that men and women are both emotional beings, although they tend to display their emotions in different ways; men and women are both nurturing beings, although they tend to do their nurturing in different ways; and men and women both value relationship, although they tend to create connection and intimacy in different ways, creates a bridge of acceptance that is important for developing relationships between men and women.

Seeing the Male Perspective: A Transformative Exercise

In your journal, write down all of the ways that you have experienced men as different from women. Do you judge any of these observations? Ask yourself: How might I shift my thinking in a particular area from believing that men are "less than," to one that sees men as "different from." For example, when it comes to nurturing children, do you say to yourself that most men are not as good at taking care of children as are women, or do you say that men nurture their children differently? Also in your journal, answer the following questions: In the past, when I have expressed my disapproval to men, was it based on my own definition of the way I thought things should be? How often have I been open to understanding—from his point of view—a man's actions, opinions, and feelings?

It is important that men and women together have conversations that acknowledge their differences and that together they find ways to accommodate both perspectives. When women communicate their willingness to accept differences, men begin to see their capability to create a relationship that is affirming, positive, and nonconfrontational. This impression nurtures the way for love, respect, and intimacy.

Taking Charge of the Neediness within Ourselves

When divorced men who are open to dating and finding a new partner have been asked what turns them off the most about a woman, they consistently answer, "neediness." Following are some of their definitions regarding a "needy" woman. Does any of it describe your behavior?

- ◆ She wants to talk on the telephone a lot.

- ◆ She seems incapable of spending any time on her own.

- ◆ She wants continual reassurance that the relationship is OK.

- ◆ After only a few dates she wants all of my time.

- ◆ I am her only interest.

- ◆ She wants me to take care of her; she can't solve problems on her own.

- ◆ Her entire life is about the relationship; she doesn't care about anything else.

- ◆ She is continually jealous of any contact that I have with other women, including my colleagues.

There is something to be learned in all feedback, even perspectives with which you do not totally agree. Therefore, even if at first blush you do not consider yourself to be needy, you might want to explore the relevance of these men's thoughts. One key to creating intimacy is understanding another person's reality and then finding a way to blend it with yours. Dismissing another person's viewpoints creates distance.

To what degree do you stop involvement with special hobbies, decrease time with friends, and stop attending to some of your own needs when you are in relationship with a man? Do you feel lonely, incomplete, or inadequate when you are not in a relationship or in the presence of your significant other? Your honest responses to these questions will reveal any tendencies that you may have to create relationships based on dependency instead of mutuality.

Psychological Possibilities: A Transformative Exercise

In your journal, write down the previous statements about neediness that were quoted from men. Under what circumstances does each one describe you? Notice that the question is not asking if these statements describe you. Rather, challenge yourself to accept that each statement may hold a piece of truth about you in some circumstances, and see if there is anything for you to learn from those occasions. For example, under what circumstances do you become jealous? When you are, what are you thinking and feeling? What do you need from your male partner during those instances? If you knew, with no doubt, that your relationship was safe, secure, and in no jeopardy, would you still feel jealous? They key in this exploration is to discern whether you feel or act needy (according to the male's feedback) because of your own insecurities, or because of a behavior on his part that is inconsistent with the understanding that you have about the definition of your relationship.

As you thoroughly consider the relevance of each of the statements of male feedback, you may notice that there are two truths triggering your feelings of, in this example, jealousy: (1) You do feel insecure when he talks frequently about his female colleague (this is something for you to explore and transform); and (2) the amount of time that he spends talking about the incredible talents of his colleague overshadows how much time he spends talking about his appreciation of your strengths (this is something for the couple to explore and transform). Embracing your individual learning pieces will help you grow and become stronger as a woman. Initiating discussion about issues that concern the thoughts, behavior, and actions of both members of a couple will strengthen the relationship.

To further pursue your own self-education on this issue, in your journal complete the following two sentences with as many true phrases as you can. Really challenge yourself to create multiple responses:

1. I feel secure in a relationship with a man when. . . .

2. I feel insecure in a relationship with a man when. . . .

As you reflect on each of your answers, see if you can identify a portion of each situation that you can work on and transform. You will obtain the most benefit from this exercise when you focus on yourself and your behavior, thoughts, and feelings, and not on the actions of men or the man in your life.

Creating lasting, meaningful intimacy requires that men and women engage in a very delicate dance between their identities as whole, distinct individuals and their desire to grow a new entity—the relationship—that weaves together the best parts of two people. Accomplishing this feat in a way that maximizes individuality and connection is a challenge you face in relationship. As women may tend to err on the side of overconnecting, overidentifying with being a part of a couple, and overinvolvement with a partner, it behooves you to develop an awareness of the part of you who feels as if she needs a connection to feel whole and alive. This awareness will enable you to shift your internal motivation from needing a relationship to desiring and enjoying the state of relating, which allows you to create intimacy that is strong, enriching, and engaging.

Discerning Love versus Falling in Love

How did you make the decision to marry your former spouse? What criteria did you use to decide that he was "the one?" If you are like many women, you may say something like: "I fell in love." "I just felt he was the right one." "One day he asked me and I just said yes." "We had been dating for a while, we had a lot in common, and so we got married." Or, "Well, we were young, what did we know?"

Whether it was because of youth, inexperience with relationships, or lack of knowledge about how to choose a mate, many women use feelings as their only criteria for selecting the person to marry. Sadly, many women, even those who are separated from their second marriage, utilize emotional decision making to choose a mate, only to find themselves in a relationship that is lacking.

Among the hardest points for transformation in this regard is to accept the notion that mate selection must not be a romantic process alone. This is true, even though the drama of "falling in love" is one of the dreams that most of women grow up with as little girls. Novels, movies, and television shows teach women to value love in partnership above all other features. The problem with this emphasis is that love and romance can sometimes be created by a setting—a beautiful sunset, soft music, an elegant meal—and can cause a wonderful sense of joy and rapture. Instead of accurately attributing this feeling to the ambiance, you may mistakenly attribute it to the person with whom you are spending the moment. Some women mistake need for love. The unconscious, for example, can be misguided and cause you to feel what you think is love when, in fact, you are experiencing fond feelings similar to those you had or wish you had with a parent.

Even the phrase "falling in love" describes love as a random act that, unfortunately, often results in people landing on the ground bruised, wounded, and bleeding. A preferred metaphor is "stepping into love," which connotes a thoughtful, contemplative, deliberate, and conscious action.

How is intimacy created if love is taken out of the equation? Love doesn't have to be removed, it just needs to be repositioned so that it becomes the entrance requirement to considering a potential mate and not the only or major factor that you take into account when deciding to mate or marry. In this way, love acts as the first step of your decision-making process. Feeling the core emotion of love is the first building block on which you initiate more extensive consideration of long-term partnering satisfaction potential. Additional questions about compatibility include:

- Do we get up in the morning at the same time?
- Do we like similar foods?
- Do we have similar money-spending and saving habits?
- Do we have compatible beliefs with respect to religion, children, and extended family?
- Do we relax in similar ways?
- Do we like similar kinds of people and enjoy socializing in similar ways?
- Are our cleanliness habits compatible?

It is also important that you ask yourself more personal questions such as:

- Do I like the way this man connects with me?
- Do I like the way this man relates to those I care about?
- Do I respect his value system?

Susan Piver, in her book *The Hard Questions: 100 Essential Questions to Ask before You Say "I Do"* (2000), agrees with the notion of putting your intellect into overdrive before making a life commitment. In her book, she provides a thought-provoking, creative, and exhaustive list of questions that can help you move beyond the feelings of love and begin to focus on issues of compatibility that are essential for growing old with someone in a loving, meaningful way.

What Do You Believe? A Transformative Exercise

As you have done with other Pillars of your life, it is important to create a vision that comprises the characteristics of the man you believe will be the best partner for you. This will be a person with whom you can create a loving and respectful relationship, and also someone with whom you can easily attend to life's daily chores, challenges, and opportunities.

Dedicate a portion of your journal to this thorough contemplating process. Your vision of the qualities that are the best match for you will develop over time. Consider this part of your journal a *contemplation in progress.* Keep your journal beside you as you meet men and as you read books about relationships. What various characteristics comprise a strong partnership that fits your own philosophies and style? What are your experiences of meeting men teaching you about what is important to you? Be sure to personalize the information that you read; record those items that are compelling to you. You may also want to interview friends and family. Ask them about their experiences choosing a mate and living with a mate. What do they wish that they had considered before getting married? Are there any attributes of their partner that they now realize are important that they may not have enjoyed earlier in their relationship?

When you have studied and extensively explored the constellation of your future mate, try this assignment: Write an advertisement looking for a friend, lover, partner, or soulmate. Using whatever length and style you need to powerfully and accurately communicate your desires, describe the man for whom you are searching. Include at least one paragraph about your relationship values and preferences, a second paragraph that describes your ideal mate, and a third paragraph that attends to the relationship that you would like to create. Be prepared for this exercise to take time and effort for it to feel complete and explicit. It will also be fun as your picture of your ideal mate begins to materialize. The clearer your vision, the more you will become energized, positive, and ready to pursue your goals.

You may be surprised by how challenging it is to find the words that are clear and specific and also contain a tone that captures a sense of who you are. Once you have completed this essay in a way that you, and others with whom you share your writing, have a detailed picture of the man with whom you would like to create intimacy, as well as what partnership means to you, you are ready to move on to the process of finding him.

My Most Powerful Dating Experience

After spending a year and a half rebuilding a positive sense of myself after the ending of an eight-year relationship, I decided that I was ready to start dating. I wanted a life-long relationship. However, I was in my midforties and concerned about the effect that my age would have on my quest.

I started attempting to meet men in traditional ways: through friends, activities, attending social functions, placing an ad in personals columns, and so forth. After four months, I felt depressed, hopeless, and most of all, powerless. It felt as if there were few available men and that I had no access to meeting them. Then, one day a pop-up ad came across my computer about a "free introductory offer to try a match service where I could meet hundreds of men in my area." I had never heard of this kind of activity, and so I clicked, read, and was fascinated. The service was, in fact, a database that contained descriptions of single men and women. My task was to enter into the computer the age, profession, geographic location, hair and eye color, religion, and hobbies that I desired in a mate and, presto, names and pictures that fit my criteria would be given to me instantly.

Much to my surprise, this is exactly what happened. I spent hours reading lengthy profiles written by men who were looking for mates. I remember laughing and laughing. The idea that not only was I not alone in my desire for quality companionship, but that there were hundreds of men in my area, thousands around the country, that were in my age group and similar circumstances, was like a fantasy Christmas morning. I subscribed to the service and began about two years of Internet matching.

At first I utilized this service as interesting entertainment. As a single, working mother, I could meet men from the privacy of my home, after my children were asleep, and after work hours. The system was convenient, safe, and fun. I had active e-mail correspondences with several men, went on a few first dates, and interacted with a good number of interesting men who, on first blush, met the dating criteria that I had set. Most important to me was that I relished my sense of control over a process that felt remote, daunting, and insurmountable.

However, as weeks went by, I realized that this medium had far more to teach than it did to merely entertain. This point is very important. Now, provided with a seemingly endless stream of men to talk to, have coffee with, and even with whom to establish ongoing connections, I had an incredible opportunity to learn about myself as a woman who was seeking a successful relationship with a man. Viewed in this way, I realized that each man whom I met, whether it was for one e-mail exchange or for more extended dating, had something to teach me. I now had the perfect venue that would help me grow and try new ways of presenting myself, interacting with men, forming close ties, and experimenting with connecting in different ways. Slowly and gradually, I could effect the transformation that was necessary for me to create the kind of intimacy that would last for the rest of my life.

During the two and a half years that I utilized the match services, I felt like I was in "relationship college." I had many teachers. I learned lessons. I gained a perspective about myself, men, and relationships that will serve me the rest of my life. Many of my friends teased me that I seemed like I was conducting a job search: I stayed in touch with the service and noted new people who joined; I initiated contact with men who seemed interesting; I spent time revising my own responses to questions; I wrote many e-mails; and I fine-tuned my concept of the kind of man I was looking for. I was very active and busy and I rode on an incredible roller coaster of excitement, rejection, initial love, and disappointment. I met, in one way or another, many wonderful, fascinating men. Until one day, after having had several short-term, exclusive relationships, I found myself on a new path with a man. The work that had begun with a series of questions about my relationship vision, continued through a process of growing and changing how I felt about myself and how I built connections, and then bloomed into a relationship that I know will continue throughout the rest of my life.

If you accept all dating as a journey, an adventure that will allow you to explore and uncover parts of yourself, then you will develop the attitude that will sustain what may be a long process filled with challenges and rewards. Creating intimacy that will last is another transformative venture. Realizing that you will move toward your vision, one experience at a time, one meeting at a time, will help you open your heart to all sorts of new men and new ways of relating. Possibilities are abundant when you can greet each individual who enters your life with a curious and welcoming spirit.

Using the Model

Many women are so excited about the prospect of developing a new relationship with a man, that they prematurely jump into action and dating. As the chapters of this book have repeatedly stated, action that happens without contemplation and thorough planning will often not have the depth necessary to last. Following the steps of visioning, planning, and then acting with regards to finding a life partner, is as critical here as it is in all of the others areas listed on the Pillars of an Independent Woman's Life. The process that will allow for deep change to occur requires that you take the time to

- ♦ Thoroughly explore your strengths and vulnerabilities.

- ♦ Contemplate your values and desires.

- ♦ Craft a multifocused plan to bring new male companionship into your life.

- ♦ Constantly reflect on what you are learning and what kind of changes will best serve your future happiness.

Creating intimacy requires sustained effort: it is not likely that it will happen overnight or with the first person you date. Finally, do not lose touch with yourself as a strong, independent woman who has interests and desires in many different sectors of her life. This wholeness, this recognition that life is about all aspects of your physical, intellectual, emotional, spiritual, and relational self, is among the hardest lessons for many women to learn. And yet, it is through this recognition of yourself as a full and multifaceted being that you will be able to pursue and truly embraces life's unlimited possibilities that lead to profound meaning and joy.

Conclusion

An Incredible Destination

As I approach the last chapter of this book I realize that I am no longer sure whether writing a book is more for the reader or the writer. I have learned so much from gathering together my thoughts and experiences. As I have continued to hone my ideas and my model, I have become clearer about the various challenges that divorced women face both due to the trauma of the divorce experience as well as from the characteristic way that women think, feel, and process their life and experiences.

I am more moved than ever before by the impact that divorce has on a woman's psyche regardless of the circumstances of the decision to divorce. And I am concerned about how, at any age, many—and perhaps most—women are ill prepared to pursue whole and meaningful lives as independent, flourishing adults. As a global community of divorced women who can now be connected and communicate with one another through all kinds of technological vehicles—such as e-mail, the World Wide Web, and telephone, as well as via traditional ways such as this book—we, as a group, can bind together and transform our circumstances.

More than ever, it is important for divorced women facing the unknown future to have time to contemplate the past, reconnect with the dreams that they have held all of their lives, and set out on a new path feeling clear, energized, and empowered. For a woman to do this successfully on her own requires a great deal of support. She needs support both from her community, especially during the inevitable down and lonely times, as well as from a coach who can help her let go of the past, create clarity about the future, and then launch ahead.

One woman beautifully described her transformative time post-divorce like this: "It is like you are a performer on a trapeze. You are moving through the air on one swing and then suddenly realize that another swing is coming. You watch for its approach, as you want to time your leap just right. Then you reach for the new bar and suddenly realize that you need to let go of the old one. Panic sets in. That moment when you are not holding on to either swing is frightening. You absolutely need to have a safety net below, or letting go and catching the next swing feels perilous."

It is difficult for women to find the support that they need. The world often seems ambivalent about whether and how to integrate divorced women into the fabric of traditional interconnections and activities, and, as a result, seems to turn a blind eye to the existence of divorced women. As a result, we seem to live in a segregated society where divorced and married people, at least socially, and often times economically, live separate lives. Divorced women describe their existence as isolated—a circumstance that they often exacerbate by not reaching out even to one another. If you make only one change because of reading this book, let it be in this area. Reach out and build relationships with other divorced women. These connections hold some of the solutions to our greatest challenges, especially the strain on time and money, companionship, and encouragement. Sharing, helping, and supporting one another will make monumental differences in all divorced women's capacity to move through this difficult time.

My heart is alive with the belief that we can change the heaviness of the event of divorce by shifting the way in which we think about it. While divorce does end one phase of our life, it also gives birth to another. While divorce does mean that we will not pursue our life dreams with one particular man and living in one particular set of circumstances, it does create an opening to embrace our passions in even more satisfying ways, with people and activities that may be better equipped and more disposed to propel our dreams to even grander heights. And, while divorce does cause us to reevaluate, rethink, and revise many of our beliefs, it gifts us with the opportunity to transform our thinking and focus our energies in new, more rewarding directions. These can be destinations that, before the divorce, we never dared to approach or imagine. Divorce can be a time of desolation. It can also be a time to accomplish unlimited possibilities if you dare to dream, gather together courage, and leap into action.

While you may not have had the power to determine many of the details of your divorce, you do have the power to choose how to proceed now. Do not minimize how you conceptualize your options. The reality that you are older, more experienced, and wiser than you were on the day that you made the decision to become married, means that you possess a strength and a capacity to impact your life that you have never had before. If you are willing to walk this new path one step at a time, and meet each roadblock with the spirit of challenge ("It is not impossible to get over this mountain, I just have to figure out how"), you can travel toward an incredible destination.

Ten Guiding Thoughts for the Journey Ahead

When I arrive at the end of a book I often am overflowing with thoughts and ideas. Often, I'm incapable of recalling individual pieces of wisdom that felt so important to me at the time I was reading them. Therefore, following is a list of ten important thoughts. On a day that you quickly need to find a spark of inspiration or comfort, perhaps you can turn to this list and find a piece of wisdom that will support or guide you.

1. Divorce is a traumatic experience. Whether or not you were the initiator of the action, it scrambles your sense of your life, your relationships, and many of your core beliefs. It is important that you be gentle with yourself, that you engage in some activities that are nurturing, that you encourage yourself and resist the inclination to judge yourself harshly, and that you remind yourself that building an independent life takes time and patience.

2. While there will be many decisions and actions that will require your effort and attention, remember that your ultimate goal is not just to survive this difficult time, but to create a foundation on which you will be able to thrive and to live a life that flows from the well of your most cherished dreams.

3. Divorce will create an opening to focus your attention in new directions. Use this shift to transform your entire life. Do not succumb to the temptation to focus on the next relationship, or on any one part of your life. See this as an expansive opportunity, a time to delve into parts of yourself that for whatever reason you did not address during your marriage.

4. A turning point of this journey involves your identity—the transformation from thinking of yourself as a part of a couple, to affirming yourself as a strong, independent woman. Feeling comfortable with this shift may take time. Ultimately, incorporating this independent spirit will allow you to meet challenges with confidence and vitality.

5. Be prepared to be anxious. This is a part of the growth process. Change the way you think about feeling edgy or nervous. Instead of believing that anxiety signals that you are not safe and should retreat to your comfort zone, realize that, most often, this feeling is a cue that you are on your growing edge—a wonderful spot that is the threshold to new experiences. Try not to flee when you become frightened or uncertain, rather, move forward. Encourage yourself. Remind yourself that you are a courageous, transforming woman who is claiming her right to live a full, fantastic, and meaningful life. You can do it!

6. Connection with other women is vitally important. Seek out opportunities to meet new women, share common activities, and give one another support. Include all women you meet as a part of your support circle. Find a point of similarity between yourself and each woman you meet. You do not have to be best friends to enjoy a woman's company. The broader and larger your support system, the stronger will be your base of support.

7. Your ability to create a life that is successful will be based on the clarity you are able to receive from the past. Review your marriage and any other relevant parts of your past. Search for ways that you may have inhibited your growth or made choices which, in retrospect, were not productive or nurturing. Take these lessons to heart and build your future on an understanding of new ways, new ideas, and new feelings about yourself and your life.

8. Bitterness, anger, disappointment, and frustration about the past, particularly toward your former spouse, is natural, but may bind you to the past more than motivate you to move ahead. The more you can let go of what was, the more tolerance you can develop for the imperfections and annoyances of people from your past, and the more energy you will have to leap into the future.

9. There are three key steps to creating transformation—each is essential. They are: vision, plan, and act. Engaging yourself fully in these activities allows you to move forward deliberately with clarity and strength. Develop a plan. Put it in writing. Post it where you can see it and refer to it often. Make a daily practice of reviewing your plan and deciding what steps you can and are willing to take each day. Your battle cry is, "One step at a time. One day at a time." Having a plan will enable you to move forward with resolve. Utilizing the support of a coach will help you achieve the clarity and drive that it is often difficult to develop on your own.

10. Your dreams are sacred. Your dreams comprise the spark within you that will ignite the fire of new possibilities. Use this time to reconnect with the dreams that you had as a child as well as the desires that sat silently during your marriage. Allow yourself to relish the joy that these dreams provide you and then transform them from imaginative fantasies to tangible goals toward which you will journey each day. Affirm yourself as an adult woman who has the power to create her reality. Commit yourself to creating the life that you have always wanted and refuse to stop reaching and moving forward until you have arrived at the destination that calls to you from within the depth of your being.

You Are Not Alone

As you finish this book, imagine yourself in a large beautiful room, seated in a very comfortable chair. You are relaxed and energized. As you look around the room there are many other women, also sitting in plush chairs, also reading, wondering, and becoming ready to take action in their lives. In many ways, this vision is reality. Given the growing numbers of divorced women around the world, it is important to realize that you are not alone. The journey, challenges, and aspirations that face and await you are a state of mind that you have in common with many other women. Every time you allow yourself to access the imagination of many women striving to move on to the next stage of their lives, all with unique circumstances and yet all with the desire to transform their existence and create authentic happiness, you may find that your sense of your own strength will multiply. You are not alone. If one woman can turn her dreams into a reality, then it is possible for us all. In this book you have heard pieces of my story as well as those of other women. We have struggled. We have doubted. We have found strength to take one step at a time. You can, too.

And We Live Happily Ever After

I believe that within each girl and within each woman is a longing to be a fairytale heroine where the story ends with the words "happily ever after." At least, this has always been true for me. The misleading message in the stories that we read in our childhood, however, is that if we wait long enough, our prince will come and provide the future of our dreams. It is important for us, as women, to remember that in many of these tales the female is asleep or bewitched. If there is a gift in divorce, which I believe there is, it is the lesson that we cannot grow or survive if we stay asleep. Divorce is our wake-up call. It is time to wake up and take charge of and create the life that we have always wanted.

There is no doubt that we can have a happy ending to our stories. The key is to realize that the fairy godmother lives within us and that the enchanted wand exists in our own capacities to take action. The magic of our cherished tales is indeed around us all the time when we allow ourselves to believe in our own powers to create and make what we once only imagined into a life that is real and lived every single day.

Bibilography

Austin, Linda. 2000. *What's Holding You Back?* New York: Basic Books.

Dean, Ben. 2000. "The Pillars Exercise: An Assessment Tool for Coaches." Bethesda, Maryland: MentorCoach Training Program.

Bridges, William. 1980. *Transitions: Making Sense of Life's Changes.* Reading, Massachusetts: Addison-Wesley.

Bridges, William. 1991. *Managing Transitions: Making the Most of Change.* New York: Perseus Books.

Deida, David. 1995. *Intimate Communion.* Deerfield Beach, Florida: Health Communications, Inc.

Duerk, Judith. 1990. *Circle of Stones: Woman's Journey to Herself.* San Diego: LuraMedia.

Fritz, Robert. 1984. *The Path of Least Resistance.* New York: Fawcett Columbine.

Gilligan, Carol. 1993. *In a Different Voice: Psychological Theory and Women's Development.* Boston: Harvard University Press.

Goleman, Daniel, Richard Boyatzis, and Annie McKee. 2002. *Primal Leadership: Realizing the Power of Emotional Intelligence.* Boston: Harvard Business School Press.

Gordon, Sol. 1990. *Why Love Is Not Enough.* Avon, MA: Adams Media Corp.

Hughes, Langston. 1995. *The Collected Poems of Langston Hughes,* edited by Arnold Rampersad and David Roessell. New York: Knopf Publishing Group.

Klauser, Henriette Anne. 2000. *Write It Down, Make It Happen.* New York: Simon & Schuster.

Lunden, Joan. 2001. *Wake-Up Calls.* New York: McGraw-Hill.

Maslow, Abraham. 1987. *Motivation and Personality,* 3rd ed. New York: Harper & Row.

Miller, Jean Baker. 1997. *The Healing Connection: How Women Form Relationships.* Boston: Beacon Press.

Piver, Susan. 2000. *The Hard Questions: 100 Essential Questions to Ask before You Say "I Do."* Los Angeles: J. P. Tarcher, Inc.

Prochaska, James O., John C. Norcross, and Carlo C. DiClemente. 1994. *Changing for Good: A Revolutionary Six-Stage Program for Overcoming Bad Habits and Moving Your Life Positively Forward.* New York: Avon Books.

Quinn, Robert E. 1996. *Deep Change: Discovering the Leader Within.* San Francisco: Jossey-Bass.

Whitmont, Edward C. 1979. *The Symbolic Quest.* Princeton: Princeton University Press.

 **Karen Kahn Wilson, Ed.D.,** is an executive/personal coach and licensed clinical psychologist who is committed to helping women maintain a positive and constructive focus in their lives. She has worked with hundreds of divorced women, helping them to see the challenges of relationships as "cycles" of potential growth. Dr. Wilson maintains a successful executive, personal and divorce coaching practice with clients throughout the US and internationally. Visit her at www.divorcedliving.com

Some Other
New Harbinger Titles

Helping Your Depressed Child, Item 3228 $14.95

The Couples's Guide to Love and Money, Item 3112 $18.95

50 Wonderful Ways to be a Single-Parent Family, Item 3082 $12.95

Caring for Your Grieving Child, Item 3066 $14.95

Helping Your Child Overcome an Eating Disorder, Item 3104 $16.95

Helping Your Angry Child, Item 3120 $17.95

The Stepparent's Survival Guide, Item 3058 $17.95

Drugs and Your Kid, Item 3015 $15.95

The Daughter-In-Law's Survival Guide, Item 2817 $12.95

Whose Life Is It Anyway?, Item 2892 $14.95

It Happened to Me, Item 2795 $17.95

Act it Out, Item 2906 $19.95

Parenting Your Older Adopted Child, Item 2841 $16.95

Boy Talk, Item 271X $14.95

Talking to Alzheimer's, Item 2701 $12.95

Helping a Child with Nonverbal Learning Disorder or Asperger's Syndrome, Item 2779 $14.95

The 50 Best Ways to Simplify Your Life, Item 2558 $11.95

When Anger Hurts Your Relationship, Item 2604 $13.95

The Couple's Survival Workbook, Item 254X $18.95

Loving Your Teenage Daughter, Item 2620 $14.95

The Hidden Feeling of Motherhood, Item 2485 $14.95

Parenting Well When You're Depressed, Item 2515 $17.95

Thinking Pregnant, Item 2302 $13.95

Call **toll free, 1-800-748-6273,** or log on to our online bookstore at **www.newharbinger.com** to order. Have your Visa or Mastercard number ready. Or send a check for the titles you want to New Harbinger Publications, Inc., 5674 Shattuck Ave., Oakland, CA 94609. Include $4.50 for the first book and 75¢ for each additional book, to cover shipping and handling. (California residents please include appropriate sales tax.) Allow two to five weeks for delivery.

Prices subject to change without notice.